Charles R. Brown

The Government of Michigan

Its history and jurisprudence

Charles R. Brown

The Government of Michigan
Its history and jurisprudence

ISBN/EAN: 9783337314484

Printed in Europe, USA, Canada, Australia, Japan

Cover: Foto ©Suzi / pixelio.de

More available books at **www.hansebooks.com**

THE

Government of Michigan,

ITS HISTORY AND JURISPRUDENCE.

ALSO, A BRIEF OUTLINE OF THE

Government of the United States.

By CHARLES R. BROWN.

SECOND EDITION, REVISED AND CORRECTED
BY THE AUTHOR.

PUBLISHED BY MOORE & QUALE,
KALAMAZOO, MICHIGAN.

1874.

TABLE OF CONTENTS.

GOVERNMENT OF MICHIGAN.

GOVERNMENT OF THE UNITED STATES.

PREFACE.

The object of this work is to supply a want long felt and now fully recognized by the people. Books have been written on the science of government, which have gained admittance into our schools; and many of our youth have, in this way, acquired much valuable information. They have learned some of the first lessons of civil government, and have been made acquainted with an outline of the government of the United States, but as yet they have not been supplied with that information concerning our own State Government, and our own responsibilities and duties so important to enable us to act well our part as citizens.

If the succeeding pages of this work shall serve to impart a knowledge of our civil jurisprudence, and of the framework and machinery of our State Government, if they shall furnish an insight into our political institutions, then surely it will inspire in the hearts of those who study them, a devotion to those institutions; and the more we know of them, the more shall we admire the wisdom and appreciate the statesmanship of the great and good men whose business it was to lay broad and deep the foundations upon which we, as a State, have built and are building.

The demand for a second edition, within two months from the time when the first was issued, has encouraged the author to revise the work. It is hoped that the historical sketch, and other matter which has been added to this edition, will greatly enhance its value and usefulness as a text-book.

To J. E. Scripps, editor of the *Detroit Evening News*, the author is indebted for a portion of the matter embraced in the historical sketch ; and to W. S. George, editor of the *Lansing Republican*, for the matter of which the chapter relative to the names of the counties is composed.

In preparing the following work, the author has consulted with a number of prominent educators in the State, as to the best plan for presenting the matter contained therein. While all agree that it is desirable, in writing a text-book, to employ such language as shall be comprehended by the youngest student, yet, on the whole, it is believed to be better in a work of this kind, to use ordinary language, and even technical terms when such are used in the law books to which we have occasion to refer. These words and terms must, sooner or later, be comprehended; and, in the judgment of the author, it would be unwise to attempt to exclude them. But, for the benefit of the younger students, it has been thought advisable to print all words, the definition or meaning of which it is conceived may not readily occur to them, in *italics*. The definition of most of the words printed in *italics* will be given in an *appendix* arranged in alphabetical order, and to which the student can easily refer. This reference, it is believed, will tend to fix the definition in the memory.

Some objection has been made to the introduction of questions, and that upon the ground that they are often so suggestive of the answer as to enable the pupil to respond correctly, though he may not have fully mastered the text. All this is true when the questions are leading; but when this is avoided and the questions are so framed as to merely call attention to the subject under consideration, they serve a most valuable purpose. Those things which the author deems important, are thus suggested to the teacher, who, in too many instances, it is feared, would otherwise pass over them without proper consideration.

GOVERNMENT OF MICHIGAN.

[For the definition of most of the words printed in *italics*, see appendix.]

CHAPTER I.

HISTORY OF MICHIGAN.

MICHIGAN, ORIGIN OF THE NAME — EXPLORATIONS AND LABORS OF THE FRENCH JESUITS.

In the language of the Chippewa tribe of Indians, the word *Mitchaw*, signifies great, and *Sagiegan*, a lake. These words were applied by the members of that tribe to lakes Michigan and Huron, which were supposed to be one lake. The land which these lakes so nearly surrounded was called *Michsawgyegan*, meaning the Lake country; and from this word, Michigan derived its name.

The country constituting the present State of Michigan, was partially explored by some French *explorers* as early as the year 1610. In 1632, Father Sagard visited the country along the shores of Lake Huron. In 1634, a party of Indians belonging to the Huron tribe, visited Quebec, a walled city in Canada. On their return they were accompanied by the *Jesuits*, Brebœuf and Daniel, who located upon the shore of

Lake Iroquois, a bay of Lake Huron, and instructed the natives in religious matters.

In 1641, a number of French Jesuits paddled a bark canoe from the St. Lawrence river up through the Ottawa river, thence crossing over to Lake Nipissing, thence down the French river to the Georgian bay, and passing the islands of Lake Huron, they reached the Falls of St. Mary, where they established a *Mission*.

In 1660, Rene Mesnard attempted an exploration of the territory around Green Bay and Lake Superior. In October of that year, he reached a bay on the south shore of Lake Superior, which he called St. Theresa. After remaining there for about eight months, he was lost in the forest. His *breviary* and *cassock* were subsequently discovered among the *amulets* of the Sioux, by whom he was probably murdered.

In 1666, Father Allouez established a mission at the Falls of St. Mary, now called Sault Ste. Marie, where, in 1668, he was joined by Fathers Dablon and Marquette. In the course of the next three years they explored the country along the shores of Lake Michigan, making the entire circuit of that lake. In 1671, Marquette built a chapel at Mackinaw, formerly called Michilimackinac, also Mackinac.

In 1673, Father Marquette and Joliet sailed through the Straits of Mackinaw on their way to discover the Mississippi. They were followed, six years later, by Robert de la Salle, who built and navigated the Griffin, a bark of sixty tons burden — the first vessel that ever floated on the northwestern lakes. The Griffin had on board Louis Hennepin, the missionary, and a party of fur-traders, who landed at *Michilimackinac*, and erected a fort and established a trading post.

___

Questions—From what did Michigan derive its name? In what year and by whom was Michigan first explored? Give the dates and particulars of the visits of Sagard, Brebœuf and Daniel. State what was done by certain French Jesuits in 1641. What is said of Rene Mesnard? Of Allouez, Dablon and Marquette? Of Marquette and Joliet? Of de la Salle and those who accompanied him?

CHAPTER II.

FRENCH MISSIONARIES AND TRADERS — ESTABLISHMENT OF MILI-
TARY AND TRADING POSTS — SURRENDER OF THE TERRI-
TORY TO THE ENGLISH — THE PONTIAC WAR.

In the fall of 1679, La Salle and his men went to Green Bay and procured a cargo of furs and dispatched them in the Griffin for Niagara. But the vessel was lost on the voyage.

From Michilimackinac, La Salle, and fourteen of his men, paddled their canoes up Lake Michigan to the mouth of the St. Joseph river, where they erected a rude fort.

In July, 1701, Antoine de la Cadillac, with a Jesuit missionary and one hundred men, located at the present site of Detroit, and commenced a permanent settlement. Here they erected a stockade which they named Fort Ponchertrain.

The forts erected at Green Bay, Ste. Marie, St. Joseph, Michilimackinac, Fort Gratiot, Detroit, and other points were designed as outposts by which the claim of the French to govern the territory could be supported, and the traders and missionaries be protected.

Prior to 1760, France claimed all of Canada, Illinois, and to the borders of the Mississippi, while the English occupied most of the country east of the Alleghany mountains. Both countries desired *supremacy* over the northern portion of the New World, and a fierce struggle between them ensued. In November, 1760, Detroit, Michilimackinac, and all the posts within the government of Canada that were in the possession of the French, were surrendered to the Crown of England.

While some of the Indians cheerfully acquiesced in the change from the rule of the French to that of the English, a large proportion of them were dissatisfied and still retained a strong friendship for the French government; and in the month of May, 1763, a *simultaneous* attack was made upon the Forts of Le Bœuf, Venango, Presque Isle, Michilimack-inac, St. Joseph, Miami, Green Bay, Ouiatonon, Pittsburgh, Sandusky, Niagara and Detroit. This attack resulted in a most frightful massacre at each of these points; Detroit, Pittsburgh and Niagara being the only places that did not fall into the hands of the savages.

Pontiac, an Ottawa chief, who lived on Pechee Island, about eight miles above the city of Detroit, was at this time the most prominent and influential leader among the Indians. Hence this war is known in history as the Pontiac war.

The siege of Detroit by Pontiac continued for eleven months, when the post was relieved by Gen. Bradstreet, with an army of three thousand men.

———

Questions—What is said of La Salle and his men? Of Antoine de la Cadillac and the Jesuit missionaries? For what purpose were the forts at the different points erected? Prior to 1760, what territory in this region was claimed by France? What was occupied by the English? What occurred in 1760? In 1763? What is said of Pontiac? Of the siege of Detroit?

CHAPTER III.

INDIAN HOSTILITIES — MICHIGAN AND THE NORTHWESTERN
TERRITORY — WAR OF 1812.

During the war of the Revolution, the Indians within the territory now comprising the present State of Michigan, were induced to make war upon the American settlements in New York, Pennsylvania, and Virginia.

In the treaty of peace of 1783, at the close of the Revolutionary War, there was no express *stipulation* for the surrender of the northwestern posts, although the territory embracing them was clearly embraced within the treaty. Notwithstanding this, the British Government continued in possession of them until 1796.

The Territory of Michigan was *organized* in 1805. For sometime previous to that date, it had formed a part of the Northwestern Territory, and the present State of Michigan formed a single county, called Wayne. The seat of Government was at Chillicothe, in the present State of Ohio, to which place the county sent a representative until 1800, when Indiana was erected into a separate territory; and two years afterwards, it was annexed to this new-formed territory, and remained under its jurisdiction until 1805.

In 1812, war was declared between the United States and Great Britain. The chief causes of this war, were, the *impressment* of American seamen, the capture of American vessels, and the enforcement of illegal blockades by the English Government.

On the 12th of July, 1812, General Hull, in command at

Detroit, surrendered to the British under General Brock. General Harrison, soon after, sent General Winchester into Michigan at the head of a thousand men, with a view to the recapture of Detroit. January 19, 1813, Winchester was attacked at Frenchtown, on the river Raisin, by the British General Proctor, with a force of two thousand British and Indians. Winchester was taken prisoner, and his entire detachment surrendered, Proctor assuring them that he would protect them from the savages. He, however, withdrew his troops to Malden, leaving his prisoners to be massacred by the Indians.

On the 10th of September of the same year, Commodore Perry defeated the British at the battle of Lake Erie ; and on the 5th of October, General Harrison defeated the British and Indians at the battle of the Thames. At this battle, the renowned chief, Tecumseh, was in command of the Indian warriors, and fought with wonderful courage and desperation. After the British had fled, Tecumseh, with his Indian warriors, engaged in a hand-to-hand conflict with Colonel Johnson and his force of mounted Kentuckians; but soon fell, pierced by a pistol ball. It is said that during the latter years of his life, " he was almost incessantly engaged either in council, or at the head of his warlike bands," and that " he sank at last on the field of his glory, with tomahawk in hand, and the cry of battle upon his lips."

> " Like monumental bronze, unchanged his look,
> A soul which pity touch'd, but never shook ;
> Train'd from his tree-rock'd cradle to his bier,
> The fierce extremes of good and ill to brook ;
> Unchanging, fearing but the shame of fear,
> A stoic of the woods, a man without a tear."

Immediately after the battle of the Thames, the British surrendered Detroit to the Americans, but retained the possession of Mackinac until December 24, 1814, when peace was concluded.

Questions - During the war of the Revolution, what was done by the Indians of Michigan? What is said in relation to the treaty of peace? Of Michigan and the Northwestern Territory? Of Indiana? State some of the chief causes of the war of 1812. When and to whom did Gen. Hull surrender Detroit? State the particulars and result of Gen. Winchester's campaign. When, by whom, and with what result was the battle of Lake Erie fought? Battle of the Thames? What is said of Tecumseh?

CHAPTER IV.

MICHIGAN AS A TERRITORY — THE UNIVERSITY — TREATIES WITH THE INDIANS — GOVERNOR AND JUDGES — LEGISLATIVE COUNCIL.

The government of the Territory of Michigan, until 1823, was vested in the Governor and Judges, who, in addition to the powers usually exercised by such officers, exercised legislative functions.

In 1817, the Governor and Judges passed an act for the establishment of what was styled the _Catholepestemiad_, or University of Michigan; although it was not until shortly after the Territory had been admitted as a State, that the present University was really established.

In 1818, all the territory lying north of Illinois and Indiana was annexed to Michigan.

In 1819, General Cass, who was then Governor of the Territory, effected a treaty with the Indians, at Saginaw, by which they relinquished their claim to 6,000,000 acres of land in the eastern part of the Territory.

In 1821, a treaty was made at Chicago, by which the Indian title to all the lands in the Territory, south of the Grand river, was relinquished. By the treaty of Greenville, concluded in 1795, the Indians had agreed that all the lands which they had granted to the French or English should be transferred to the United States.

In 1823, Congress abolished the act conferring legislative power upon the Governor and Judges, and provided for the establishment of a Legislative Council, to consist of nine members. The members of the Council were appointed by the President of the United States, who selected them from eighteen persons chosen by the people. In 1825, the Council was made to consist of thirteen members. In 1827, the Council was made elective by the people.

In 1831, General Cass was appointed Secretary of War, and George B. Porter of Pennsylvania, was appointed Governor of the Territory. He died in 1834, whereupon Stevens T. Mason, Secretary of the Territory, became acting Governor.

Questions — What is said of the government of the Territory prior to 1823? What was done by the Governor and Judges in 1817? What Territory was annexed to Michigan in 1818? What is said of the treaty of 1819? Of 1821? Of 1795? What is said of the Legis- lative Council? To what office was General Cass appointed in 1831? Who succeeded him as Governor? Who succeeded Governor Porter?

CHAPTER V.

THE TOLEDO WAR — SETTLEMENT OF THE DIFFICULTY BY
CONGRESS.

By the Ordinance of 1787, it was contemplated that a
line due east and west through the southern extremity of
Lake Michigan should be the dividing line between the two
tiers of States to be erected out of the Northwestern Territory. By the act of Congress establishing the Territory of
Michigan, this line was designated as its southern boundary.
Ohio, however, desired and claimed a strip of land about fifteen miles wide, north of this line ; and in 1812, Congress
recognized the line as claimed by Ohio, and in 1816 a survey
was authorized to be made accordingly. Michigan was about
to apply for admission as a State, and insisted on the line as
originally established, and made preparations to resist a party
of surveyors sent by the authorities of Ohio to re-survey the
line. The surveyors were driven off by a party of Michigan
men. Believing that Ohio would send troops to take possession of the disputed territory, acting Governor Mason called
out the militia of the Territory, and as Commander-in-Chief,
placed himself at their head, and marched "to the front."
No enemy appearing, the troops were allowed to disperse and
return to their homes. Congress finally decided the controversy in favor of Ohio, and gave to Michigan, in lieu of the
strip in dispute, about twenty-five thousand square miles of
country in what is now known as the Upper Peninsula.

Questions — What was the line originally contemplated as the
dividing line between the present State of Michigan, and the territory

2

south of it? What public acts recognized this as the line? What was the occasion for the controversy between Ohio and Michigan? State what was done by Michigan in relation to the matter. How was the difficulty finally settled?

CHAPTER VI.

MICHIGAN AS A STATE — BANKING — INTERNAL IMPROVEMENTS.

In the spring of 1835, a convention called for that purpose framed a constitution for a State Government, and application was made to Congress for the admission of the Territory as a State. In June, 1836, an act was passed admitting her upon condition that she should accept the boundary line as claimed by Ohio. On the 15th of December the convention convened to decide the question, voted to accept the proposition. January 26th, 1837, Congress passed an act recognizing Michigan as a State of the Union.

The population of the State in 1837, was estimated at two hundred thousand ; and its territory embraced about forty thousand square miles, which was divided into thirty-six counties.

In 1837, the Legislature made provision for free banking, and in less than eight months, forty-five banks were established. With the fifteen banks that had been previously chartered, the banking capital of the State amounted to $10,115,000. With the immense amount of currency thus issued, money was very cheap, and speculation ran high. Of course the inflation soon collapsed, and thousands who had imagined themselves rich, found their currency almost worthless.

In 1837, the Legislature established a Board of Commissioners on Internal Improvement, with authority to construct three railroads across the State : The Southern from Monroe to New Buffalo ; the Central from Detroit to St. Joseph ; and the Northern from Port Huron to Grand Haven. Also, three canals : The St. Mary's Ship canal ; the Clinton and Kalamazoo canal, to extend from Mt. Clemens to the mouth of the Kalamazoo river; and the Saginaw or Northern canal, to extend from Bad river to Maple river, so as to secure water communication between Saginaw and Grand Haven. The estimated cost of these improvements was over $10,000,000. To raise this sum, it was provided that the *surplus revenue* of the State, and five per cent. of the proceeds from the sale of lands belonging to the State, should be appropriated, and to effect a loan not to exceed $5,000,000, payable in twenty-five years, with interest at six per cent. per annum.

The bonds were sold, and a large proportion of the money realized was expended on the proposed works, but it was soon found that the interests of the State required that these works should be disposed of, and be carried on by private enterprise. The Central and Southern roads, on which most of the money had been expended, were sold by the State in 1846. The Clinton and Kalamazoo, and the Saginaw or Northern canals were abandoned, and the Northern road upon which some work had been done was converted into a wagon road.

J. E. Scripps, Esq., of Detroit, has prepared and published in the " Michigan State Gazetteer," a brief outline history of Michigan, in which is found some very valuable information concerning the Internal Improvement scheme, an extract from which is copied in a note to this chapter.

Questions — In what year was the State Constitution adopted? State what action was taken by Congress in regard to the admission of Michigan. What was the population of the State in 1837? Square miles of territory? What is said of banking and currency? What action was taken by the Legislature in 1837, with reference to internal improvements? What was the estimated cost of these proposed improvements? What provision was made for meeting these expenses? What disposition did the State make of these works?

NOTE.—"The first step of the board was to purchase the Detroit & St. Joseph R. R., no part of which was in operation, though considerable work had been done between Detroit and Ypsilanti. To this place it was opened for traffic February 3, 1838. Surveys on all the other works were in 1837 completed, and 30 miles of the Southern road put under contract. The total expenditures this year were $415,618.

"Meanwhile the Governor, who had been empowered by the Legislature to negotiate the $5,000,000 loan, had closed a contract with the Morris Canal and Banking company of New Jersey, by which they took the entire amount of the bonds and agreed to pay for the same, about one quarter down and the balance in quarterly instalments of $250,000 each, the bonds to be delivered at once. Three millions of these bonds they immediately turned over to the Bank of the United States, by which they were hypothecated largely in Europe. Great complaint seems to have been made at home of the Governor's recklessness in thus hastily closing so large a transaction, and in his parting with the bonds without receiving proper security for the payment. Nor was the complaint without just grounds, for in 1840, when there was still $2,158,937 due from the purchasers, it came to light that both banks were insolvent For some time the financial condition of the State was most critical, but in 1843 the Legislature passed an act authorizing the issue of new bonds for the amount that had been actually received by the State, the same to be delivered upon the surrender of the entire amount of outstanding bonds, or *pro rata* for any portion that might be surrendered. In this way the entire $5,000,000, except about $56,000, was gradually retired, and the bonds given in lieu thereof were duly paid in 1863.

"In 1838, $530,496 was expended on the Internal Improvement works, and considerable surveying and clearing was done, besides the completion of the Central railroad to Ypsilanti. In 1839 the expenditure was $693,883. The Central road was opened to Ann Arbor and the Southern to Petersburgh. An attempt to commence work on the Sault canal was defeated by a collision between the contractors and the United States officials at Fort Brady.

"In 1840 the Governor in his message to the Legislature deplored the Internal Improvement scheme, and recommended the suspension of further work, except where necessary to complete and utilize what had already been commenced. This year $463,816 was expended, the Central road being brought to within four miles of Dexter, the Southern opened to Adrian, and a heavy amount of work being done upon the Clinton & Kalamazoo canal between Mt. Clemens and Rochester. In 1841 there was expended $419,139. The Central was opened to Dexter, July 4, and was immediately pushed on to Jackson. The Southern had not got beyond Adrian. The Northern railroad, upon which considerable clearing and grading had been done, was this year ordered by the Legislature to be completed as a wagon road.

"January 1, 1842, the Central was opened to Jackson. The Southern was during this year made ready for the iron as far as Hillsdale, but the credit of the State was not at that time good enough to enable it to buy iron on credit, and cash it had none. Sixteen miles of the Clinton & Kalamazoo canal were completed at a cost of $338,330, but it had not yet been brought into use. The Legislature in January, 1842, by resolution forbade the letting of any further contracts on the public works, but provision was made for extending the Central and Southern railroads. The year 1843 saw the latter opened to Hillsdale. The expenditures in 1842 were $170,545, and in 1843 $160,416. In 1844 the Central road was opened to Marshall and graded to Kalamazoo. The Southern was this year re-built between Monroe and Adrian, the superstructure having rotted out, and the Palmyra & Jacksonburg road was purchased by the State for $22,000. This latter road had been prepared for the iron from Palmyra to Tecumseh, but had been allowed to go to decay without ever being put in full operation. The Central railroad was now earning from year to year a moderate profit over expenses, the Southern road a very trifling amount, if anything, and none of the other public works were at all productive. In 1845 the Central was finished to Battle Creek and some progress made with the reconstruction of the Tecumseh branch of the Southern. The expensiveness of keeping strap-rail. roads in repair had by this time been found to be a serious drawback to the productiveness of railroad property, and the commissioners in their report for this year suggested the importance of immediately reconstructing both roads with 'T' rail, and recommended as the only feasible method of securing the accomplishment of this enterprise, the sale of the roads to some responsible company. In this year the navigation of the Clinton & Kalamazoo canal was inaugurated by a small boat of 20 tons burden.

"On February 1, 1846, the Central road was completed to Kalamazoo; on the 23d of September its sale to the Michigan Central Railroad company was perfected, the purchase price being $2,000,000 and the payments being made in bonds and other State indebtedness. One month later the sale of the Southern road to the Michigan Southern Railroad company was consummated by the payment of the first instalment of the purchase price, which had been fixed at $500,000, payable also in State indebtedness within 10 years. By these sales the State debt was greatly diminished and the two roads placed in the hands of strong and enterprising companies, by whom they were speedily completed, and under whom they have since achieved reputations for admirable management second to those of no other railroads in the country.

"The canal still remained to the State. This was in 1846 put in navigable order between Mt. Clemens and Utica, but only $43 was received in tolls. The following year further repairs were made and an ineffectual effort made to lease the work. From this time it appears to have been wholly neglected by the State. Between Rochester and Utica it has since been utilized for water-power purposes, but below Utica it has been allowed to go wholly to decay."

CHAPTER VII.

EXTENT OF TERRITORY — RESOURCES OF THE STATE.

The total land surface of Michigan comprises an area of 56,243 square miles, while the area of its waters is computed at 36,324 square miles.

From the time when the State sold its Public Works, to the present, it has steadily progressed in wealth and population. The census of 1870 showed a population of 1,184,059, and we now have a little over 3,000 miles of railroad within the State, and a lake coast of nearly 1,500 miles.

The surface of the Upper Peninsula is rugged and hilly. It has, nevertheless, much valuable pine timber, and is, perhaps, the richest mineral region in the world, especially in copper and iron.

The upper portion of the Lower Peninsula is still covered with dense forests of pine and hard wood, though the manufacture of lumber, as a branch of industry, has for a number of years been extensively prosecuted. The soil of the Lower Peninsula is varied, and well adapted to the raising of all kinds of products that may be grown in this latitude.

In the Saginaw valley, salt is manufactured in abundance. We also have, in the State, rich mines of coal, iron, copper, and silver.

Questions — How many square miles of land has Michigan? The area of its waters? What was its population in 1870? How many miles of railroad has it? The extent of its lake coast? What is said of the Upper Peninsula? Of the Lower Peninsula?

CHAPTER VIII.

GOVERNORS OF MICHIGAN.

Under French rule the Governors of the Territory embracing the present State of Michigan, were as follows :

Sieur de Mesy, appointed in	.	1663	Marquis de Vaudreuil, . . 1703
Sieur de Courcelle, .	.	1665	Marquis de Beauharnais, . . 1726
Sieur de Frontenac,	.	1672	Sieur Compte de la Gallisoniere, 1749
Sieur de Barre, .	.	1682	Sieur de la Jonquire, . . 1749
Sieur de Marquis de Nouville,	.	1685	Marquis du Quesne de Menneville, 1752
Sieur de Frontenac,	.	1689	Sieur de Vaudreuil de Cavagnal, . 1755
Sieur Chevalier de Calliers,	.	1699	

Under the English rule the Governors were :

James Murray, appointed in	.	1765	Henry Hamilton, . . . 1774
Paulus Emilius Irving,	.	1766	Henry Hope. 1775
Guy Carleton,	.	1766	Lord Dorchester, . . . 1776
Hector T. Cramahe,	.	1770	Alured Clarke, . . . 1791
Guy Carleton,	.	1774	Lord Dorchester, . , . 1798
Frederick Haldemand,	.	1774	

The American Governors under the Territorial Government were as follows :

William Hull, appointed in	.	1805	Stevens T. Mason, . . . 1834
Lewis Cass, .	.	1814	John S. Horner, . . . 1835
George B. Porter, .	.	1832	Stevens T. Mason, . . . 1835

The following is a list of the several Governors who have served from the admission of the State into the Union, down to the present time :

	Inaugurated.	Retired.
STEVENS T. MASON, . .	Oct. 1837	Jan. 1840
WILLIAM WOODBRIDGE, .	Jan. 1840	Feb. 1841*
J. WRIGHT GORDON,† . .	Feb. 1841	Jan. 1842
JOHN S. BARRY, . . .	Jan. 1842	Jan. 1846

* Resigned upon being elected to Congress.
† Lieutenant Governor, acting as Governor.

Alpheus Felch, . . .	Jan.	1846	Mar. 1847‡
William S. Greenly,§ .	Mar.	1847	Jan. 1848
Epaphroditus Ransom, .	Jan.	1848	Jan. 1850
John S. Barry, . . .	Jan.	1850	Jan. 1852
Robert McClelland, . .	Jan.	1852	Mar. 1853**
Andrew Parsons, . .	Mar.	1853	Jan. 1855
Kinsley S. Bingham, . .	Jan.	1855	Jan. 1859
Moses Wisner, . . .	Jan.	1859	Jan. 1861
Austin Blair, . . .	Jan.	1861	Jan. 1865
Henry H. Crapo, . . .	Jan.	1865	Jan. 1869
Henry P. Baldwin, . .	Jan.	1869	Jan. 1873
John J. Bagley, · · .	Jan.	1873	Jan. 1875
John J. Bagley, . . .	Jan.	1875	

Questions — Who was the first Governor of the Territory embracing the present State of Michigan? Will you give the names of the French Governors, and the dates of their appointment from 1663 to 1685? From 1689 to 1726? From 1749 to 1755? Who was the first English Governor? Give the names of the English Governors, and the dates of their appointments? Of the American Governors, under the Territorial Government? Give the names of the Governors under the State Government.

CHAPTER IX.

MICHIGAN DURING THE REBELLION.

In the late war of the Rebellion, Michigan achieved for herself a glorious record. She sent to the field one regiment of engineers and mechanics, 11 regiments and 3 independent companies of cavalry, 14 batteries of artillery, 31 regiments

‡ Resigned on being elected U. S. Senator.
§ Lieutenant Governor, acting as Governor.
** Resigned upon being appointed Secretary of the Interior.

of infantry, and 5 companies of sharpshooters, numbering in all 90,747 men. Of these, 4,175 were killed in action or died of wounds, and 9,230 died of disease while in service.

From the beginning to the close of the war, the Michigan troops bore the reputation of being among the bravest and best disciplined in the army, and there were very few of the more important engagements where Michigan was not represented, and where her regiments were not conspicuous for the efficient aid they rendered.

Questions — How many regiments of engineers did Michigan send to the late war of the Rebellion? Of cavalry? Batteries of artillery? Regiments of infantry? Companies of sharpshooters? How many men in all? How many were killed, or died of wounds? How many died of disease? What is said of the bravery of Michigan troops?

CHAPTER X.

ORIGIN OF THE NAMES OF COUNTIES — DATES OF THEIR ORGANIZATION.

The following is taken from an account of the origin and derivation of the names of most of the counties of Michigan, by Mr. W. S. George, editor of the *Lansing Republican.* The dates in parentheses are those of the legal organization of the several counties.

Allegan (1835) — Named from an ancient Indian tribe in the Alleghanies. The word *gan* signifies Lake.

Antrim (1843) — Named from the northeastern county of Ireland.

Barry (1839) — Named from Wm. T. Barry, Postmaster-

General of the United States, in Jackson's cabinet, from 1829 to 1835. Born 1785, died 1835.

Bay (1857) — Named from its bordering on Saginaw Bay.

Benzie (1869) — Named from Aux becscies, the French designation of that important river on which the thriving village of Frankfort is situated.

Berrien (1831) — Named from John M. Berrien, Attorney-General in Jackson's cabinet from 1829 to 1831. Born 1781, died 1856.

Branch (1833) — Named from John Branch, Secretary of the Navy in Jackson's cabinet from 1829 to 1831. Born 1782, died 1863.

Calhoun (1833) — Named from John C. Calhoun, Vice-President of the United States from 1825 to 1833. Born 1782, died 1850.

Cass (1829) — Named from Lewis Cass, Territorial Governor of Michigan from 1814 to 1831, Secretary of War under Jackson, Minister to France, U. S. Senator 12 years, Secretary of State under Buchanan. Born 1782, died 1866.

Clinton (1838) — Named from De Witt Clinton, the most illustrious Governor the State of New York ever had, and projector and virtual builder of the Erie Canal. Born 1769, died 1828.

Charlevoix (1869) — Named from Pierre F. X. de Charlevoix, a French traveler and Jesuit missionary. Born 1682, died 1761.

Cheboygan (1840) — An Indian name for a river emptying into the Straits of Mackinaw from the south. The original word, *Chabwegan*, signifies a place of ore.

Chippewa (1826) — Named from a powerful Indian tribe, sometimes called " Ojibbeways."

Delta (1861) — Named from its partial resemblance in

position to the "delta" or triangular fork of land at the mouth of the river Nile in Egypt.

Eaton (1837) — Named from John H. Eaton, Secretary of War in Jackson's cabinet from 1829 to 1831. Born 1790, died 1856.

Emmet (1843) — Named from Robert Emmet, the eloquent young Irish patriot, who was one of the leaders in an insurrection against British misrule in 1803, but failed, and was hung by the government as a traitor at the age of only 23 years.

Genesee (1836) — Named from the fertile and pleasant county in Western New York, from whence many settlers emigrated to this part of Michigan. In the Seneca language, *Je-nis-hi-yuh* signified beautiful, pleasant valley, and was truly descriptive of the valley of the Genesee river.

Grand Traverse (1851) — Named from the peculiarity of the bay on which it is situated. The French sailors who ran into it, perhaps thinking it was a lake, had to sail a long distance or make a "grand traverse" to get out again.

Gratiot (1855) — Named from Fort Gratiot, which formerly stood at the foot of Lake Huron ; the early French traders fortified that point in 1688.

Hillsdale (1835) — Named from the rolling and diversified face of the country, "up hill and down dale."

Houghton (1845) — Named from Douglas Houghton, the talented geologist and first thorough explorer and describer of the mineral wealth of our Upper Peninsula, whose death by drowning in 1845 was deeply lamented.

Huron (1859) — The name of a tribe of Indians, also called "Wyandottes." A fragment of the Hurons about 1680, settled at Detroit. The slang phrase, "*Quelles hures !*" (what heads !) was applied by an astonished French traveler to the Wyandottes, on seeing their fantastic mode of dressing the hair ; with some of the warriors, it bristled in a ridge across the crown, like the back of a hyena. From *hures* was derived *Huron*.

Ingham (1838) — Named from Samuel D. Ingham, Secretary of the Treasury in Jackson's cabinet from 1829 to 1831. Born 1773, died 1860.

Ionia (1837) — Named from a province in ancient Greece, where the simple but majestic order of architecture known as " Ionic " had its origin.

Iosco (1857) — An illegitimate Indian name of which Hon. H. R. Schoolcraft was father, and of which he gave the meaning as " Water of Light."

Isabella (1859) — Named from the illustrious Queen of Spain, who nearly four centuries ago fitted out Columbus's fleet, and enabled him to discover the new world. She was born 1451, died 1504.

Jackson (1832) — Named from the iron-willed and popular President of the United States from 1829 to 1837. Born 1767, died 1845.

Kalamazoo (1830) — An Indian name, signifying " the mirage or reflecting river," applied to the stream which waters this county and parts of Calhoun and Allegan. It was originally spelled *Kikalamazoo*. It is claimed by some to have been derived from the Indian word *Ke-Kanamozoo*, or " Boiling Pot," by which name the river was sometimes called.

Kent (1836)—Named from Chancellor James Kent, the celebrated jurist of New York. Born 1763, died 1847.

Keewenaw (1861)—An Indian name, curtailed from *Kiwi-wai-non-ing*, signifying a portage, or place where a portage is made; it may mean the place where the portage ends or the canoe is " carried back " to the lake.

Lenawee (1826)—An Indian name, derived perhaps from

the Delaware *Lenno*, or rather from the Shawnee *Lenawai*, " man."

Livingston (1836)—Named from Edward Livingston, Secretary of State in Jackson's cabinet from 1831 to 1833. Born 1764, died 1836.

Mackinac (1840)—An Indian name, curtailed from *Michinimackinong*, the place of Giant Fairies, or Great Turtle place.

Macomb (1818)—Named from Gen. Alexander Macomb, who was born in Detroit, entered our regular army and won promotion, fought bravely in 1813 at Fort George and Niagara, and gained the decisive victory at Plattsburg over the British, September 11, 1814. Born 1782, died 1841.

Manistee (1840)—An Indian name for the river which Charlevoix visited over a century ago. The Indians interpret the name as " a river at whose mouth there are islands."

Manitou (1855)—An Indian name for some deity which they acknowledged. It is not very clear that they recognized only one "Great Spirit."

Marquette (1845)—Named from the Jesuit Father Jacques Marquette, an early explorer of the great lakes. Born 1637, died 1675.

Mason (1843)—Named from Stevens T. Mason, the last Territorial and first State Governor of Michigan.

Menominee (1863)—Named from an Indian tribe in Wisconsin.

Midland (1850)—Named from its central position in the Lower Peninsula.

Monroe (1817)—Named from James Monroe, President of the United States from 1817 to 1825. Born 1758, died 1831.

Montcalm (1840)—Named from the Marquis de Montcalm, that gallant commander of the French forces who was vanquished and killed at the taking of Quebec, when General Wolfe captured the city but lost his life. Born 1712, died 1759.

Muskegon (1859)—An Indian name, signifying "marshy river, or wet prairie."

Newaygo (1859)—From Indian words, signifying "great water" or "much water."

Oakland (1820)—Named from the face of the country when it was first settled by white men; "oak openings" prevailing.

Oceana (1851)—Named from its watery location on the eastern shore of Lake Michigan.

Osceola (1843)—Named from the famous chief of the Seminole Indians, who kept the Florida war going several years, baffling our whole regular army and costing the public treasury about a hundred million dollars. Born 1803, died 1838.

Ontonagon (1845)—An Indian name derived from *Nunda-norgan*, hunting river.

Ottawa (1837)—An Indian name signifying traders, and applied to a powerful tribe which once occupied Northwestern Michigan.

Saginaw (1835)—An Indian name, derived from *Sac-e-nong*, or Sac town.

Sanilac (1857)—This name is either of Indian or Canadian French origin; its meaning not ascertained. It is among the names invented by Mr. Schoolcraft.

Shiawassee (1837)—An Indian name signifying "straight running," in reference, doubtless, to the course of the river from Owosso to St. Charles.

St. Clair (1821)—Named from Lake St. Clair. Hon. Augustus B. Woodward, first Chief Justice of the Territory, believes that the lake derived its name from the French officer St. Clair, and the river from the British officer Sir John Sinclair. In the early records the name of the county is sometimes given as Sinclair. In reality both names are the same and designate a proud and ancient Scotch family of Norman origin.

St. Joseph (1829)—Named from the husband of the Virgin Mary, canonized by the Romish church, and regarded by the Jesuits as the patron saint of New France. Our Northwestern States as well as the Canadas were formerly called " New France."

Tuscola (1840)—Another of Schoolcraft's illegitimate Indian names. He gave its meaning as " Warrior Prairie," from the Muscogee *Tusca*, warrior.

Van Buren (1837) — Named from Martin Van Buren, who held the offices of Governor of New York, U. S. Senator, Secretary of State in Jackson's cabinet, Minister to England, Vice-President, and President of the United States from 1837 to 1841. Born 1782, died 1862.

Washtenaw (1836) — The Indian name of Grand river, which rises in the southwestern part of the county. The name was originally *Wash-ten-ong*, meaning *at* or *on* the river.

Wayne (1796) — Named from General Anthony Wayne, the brilliant hero of the Revolutionary army, and the victorious Indian fighter near our southeastern border. He was nicknamed " Mad Anthony," on account of his hair-brained courage and dash. The Indians gave him a name which signified *Tornado*. In the early Territorial government of Michigan, Wayne county included the whole State. Gen. Wayne was born 1745 ; died 1796, while on his way to take command at Detroit.

Wexford (1843) — Named from a maritime county in the southeastern part of Ireland.

[It is not deemed necessary to arrange questions for this chapter, as they would necessarily be nearly the same for each county. The proper questions will be readily suggested to the teacher.]

CHAPTER XI.

OF THE SURVEY OF THE PUBLIC LANDS — SUBDIVISIONS OF
TOWNSHIPS AND SECTIONS.

The lands embraced within the *territorial* limits of Michigan, had been *surveyed* by or under the direction of the Surveyor-General of the United States, before the State was admitted into the Union. The plan adopted in making this survey, was to draw two imaginary lines across the territory; one east and west, and the other north and south. The line running north and south was called the principal meridian, and the one running east and west was called the base line. The principal meridian commences on the south line of the State, between the counties of Hillsdale and Lenawee, and extends to the northern extremity of the State. The base line commences at a point in the western boundary line of the State, between the counties of Allegan and Van Buren, and extends east to the eastern boundary of the State. In making the survey of Michigan, the territory was divided into townships six miles square, and these were subdivided into thirty-six sections, of a square mile each, the townships being numbered in regular order east and west of the meridian line, and north and south of the base line. Thus, where the meridian and base lines *intersect* and cross each other, the township next north of the base line, and next east of the meridian line would be called " township number one north, in *range* number one east," while the township next east of it would be, "township number two east, in range number one north." The following *diagram* will aid in explaining this:

DIAGRAM SHOWING HOW TOWNSHIPS ARE NUMBERED WITH REFERENCE TO THE MERIDIAN AND BASE LINES.

The sections contain six hundred and forty acres each, unless they are, as is sometimes the case, fractional. Sometimes a stream or a lake occupies a large portion of a quarter-section, and the part not so occupied we call "fractional." Sometimes in measuring the townships, the surveyors would, owing to the great difficulties they had to encounter in measuring the distances through the wilderness, swamps, and lakes, and over the hills, include a little too much territory, or perhaps not quite enough. In such case, when the townships were *subdivided* into sections, and the measurements were made with more care, the subdivisions on the north and west sides of the townships were made to contain whatever was

3

left, more or less, so that all the other sections in the township should contain just six hundred and forty acres, each.
The sections are numbered, commencing at the northeast
corner of the townships, and for convenience, are subdivided
into quarters; and we frequently see lands described as a
quarter of a quarter.

The following is a plan of a township, the subdivisions
representing sections:

6	5	4	3	2	1
7	8	9	10	11	12
18	17	16	15	14	13
19	20	21	22	23	24
30	29	28	27	26	25
31	32	33	34	35	36

The United States government gave to Michigan, section
sixteen, in every township, of the public lands, for the use of
schools, and in addition thereto, seventy-two sections for the
support of the State University.

DIAGRAM OF A SECTION, SUBDIVIDED.

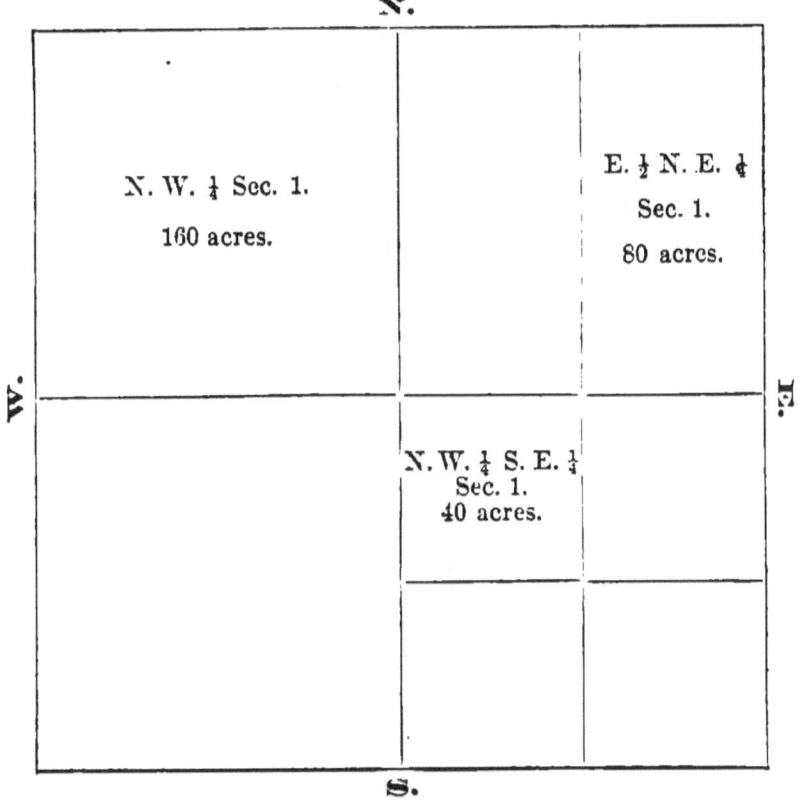

Questions—What two lines were adopted as a basis for surveying the Territory of Michigan? How was the Territory divided? How many miles square are the townships of Michigan? In what way are the Townships designated? Will you make a diagram explaining this? How are the townships subdivided? How many sections are there in a township? How are they numbered and designated? Will you make a diagram explaining this? How many acres are there in a full section? How are the sections subdivided? Are these subdivisions always uniform? In what way are some of the subdivisions made fractional? Will you illustrate the subdivisions of sections by a diagram? What is said of a *grant* from the United States of certain lands to this State?

CHAPTER XII.

OF THE ORGANIZATION OF GOVERNMENT, AND THE EXERCISE OF SOVEREIGNTY.

To enable the people to defend their rights and to do right and justice, they unite together in a *body politic;* and when the people are so united and have agreed upon certain rules by which they are to be governed, we speak of such union, in its most enlarged sense, as a State. Bouvier defines a State as follows: "In its most enlarged sense, it signifies a self-sufficient body of persons united together in one *community* for the defence of their rights and to do right and justice to *foreigners.*"

In a more limited sense, a State means the territory occupied by the united body of people, as, the State of Michigan.

In many countries the rulers are sovereign; that is, they exercise control, authority and power as they see fit, regardless of the wishes or consent of the governed. But in this country no single individual has the right to exercise this power. Here the people choose their rulers, and, by written constitutions, define and limit their powers and duties.

Sovereignty, the supreme or highest power among men, in this country, resides in the people. This power, however, the people authorize their officers to exercise, and, having *instituted* a government, they have agreed to submit to and abide by certain rules and regulations; have *conferred* power upon their officers to enforce obedience to such rules and regulations.

Government is defined as, "the manner in which sovereignty is exercised in each State."

In every State there is either some individual or body of men whose duty it is to see to the enforcement of the laws; and we sometimes refer to them as the government.

Questions—What is a State, and for what purpose is it organized? Give Bouvier's definition of a State. What is a sovereign? With whom does sovereign power reside in this country? Who exercises the power of sovereignty in this country? In what way and by what authority are the people required to submit to the power we call sovereignty? What is government? In what other sense do we sometimes use the word government?

CHAPTER XIII.

OF LAWS AND THEIR NECESSITY—RIGHTS AND DUTIES.

The rules of action adopted for the government of the people, are called laws. Hence a law is that which commands us what to do and forbids the things we are not to do.

The necessity for these rules or laws is *apparent* when we observe and consider the many differences and difficulties among men which arise either from mistakes, honest disagreements, want of judgment, or intentional misconduct or wrong. They are necessary, to indicate to us our duties as members of society, and to protect us in the enjoyment of our rights.

A right is a legal title or a just claim to anything. We have a right to life, a right to our earnings, and a right to act as we please, and to go where we please, provided we do not interfere with the rights of others.

These rights, however, are subject to certain *restrictions* or *limitations* and may be *forfeited,* or, when the public good requires it, may be taken from us. By *violating* the law we may forfeit our liberty and our property. If called upon to take up *arms* in behalf of the country, it is our duty to *respond,* and if needs be, to *surrender* our property and our lives.

As children are *dependent* upon their parents, they owe them certain duties, not the least of which is obedience to their *commands.* So with the citizen, dependent upon the State for the protection of himself and his property; he is bound to observe the rules prescribed for his conduct.

Questions—What are human laws? How is the necessity for law apparent? For what are laws necessary? What is a right? Mention some of our rights. To what are these rights subject? How may we forfeit our liberty and property? What duty do we owe the country? State one of the grounds on which obedience is a duty.

CHAPTER XIV.

OF THE DIFFERENT FORMS OF GOVERNMENT—CONSTITUTIONS, AND THE PURPOSE THEY SERVE.

Different forms of government prevail in different countries. In those countries where the power to *govern* and make the laws, is *vested* in one person, we call the government a monarchy. Where the great body of *freemen* assemble together to make the laws and to transact the b siness of the State, we call the government a democracy.

Where the chief magistrate gets his power to rule by *inheritance,* but has no power to make the laws, we call the government a mixed government, or a limited monarchy. Such is the government of Great Britain. The laws are framed by Parliament, and when approved by the monarch become *operative.*

Where the people enjoy common rights and privileges, but exercise the sovereign power by and through representatives elected by them, we call the government a republic. Every State in the American Union is a republic.

A pure democracy and our American Republic differ in this, that in the former, the citizens assemble in a body to make the laws, while in the latter, the people choose representatives to act for them. Both are governments of the people and derive their powers from them.

The form of government in each of the United States is represented by a written constitution. These constitutions are called the *fundamental* or *political* law. They are adopted as the *agreement* of the people—as the framework of the government—and *limit* the power of the various departments.

Any act of the Legislature or of any officer of the State which *conflicts* with any of the provisions of the constitution is invalid. Thus the people are protected against unjust *enactments* and *usurpation* of power by their public servants.

Questions—Are the forms of government the same in all countries? What is a monarchy? What is a democracy? What is a mixed government or limited monarchy? What form of government has Great Britain? What is a republic? What form of government have the States of the American Union? Wherein consists the difference between a democracy and a republic? From whence do republics and democracies derive their power? By what are the forms of government represented in the several States of this Union? By what names are constitutions sometimes called? What is the object or purpose of constitutions? How do they protect the people?

CHAPTER XV.

GOVERNMENT OF MICHIGAN — DIVISIONS OF THE POWERS OF
GOVERNMENT.

The powers of Government are divided into three departments: the Legislative, Executive, and Judicial.

The Legislative department is that which enacts the laws for the government of the people, and its power is vested in a Senate and House of Representatives. The Senate has thirty-two members, and the House of Representatives has one hundred members.

These officers are elected by the people, from districts into which the State is divided, and hold their offices for two years.

The Executive power of the Government is vested in a Governor, who is assisted by such other officers as are necessary to carry out and execute the laws. Indeed, it is the business of this department to see to it that the laws are carried into effect.

The Judicial department is that which administers justice according to the laws, and is composed of the different Courts of Justice. The Judges and Justices of the Peace are Judicial officers.

Questions—Into how many departments are the powers of government divided? Name them. What is the Legislative department? How many members are there in each House? How are such members elected? How long do they hold their terms of office? In whom is the Executive department vested? What is the special duty of this department? What is the Judicial department? Of what officers is this department composed?

CHAPTER XVI.

ELECTION OF STATE, COUNTY, AND TOWNSHIP OFFICERS.

In order that the government may be *administered*, it is necessary that *officers* should be elected for that purpose. As the duties of some of these officers pertain to the whole State, we call them State officers; those whose duties are limited to the county, we call county officers; and those whose duties are limited to, and *pertain* to the government of the townships, cities, and villages, we call township, city, or village officers, as the case may be.

Once in two years, on the Tuesday succeeding the first Monday in November, a general election is held throughout the State, at which the people choose, by ballot, their Governor, Lieutenant-Governor, Secretary of State, Superintendent of Public Instruction, State Treasurer, Commissioner of the Land Office, members of the State Board of Education, Auditor-General, Attorney-General, members of the Legislature, and Representatives in Congress, Sheriff, County Clerk, County Treasurer, Register of Deeds, Prosecuting Attorney, and Circuit Court Commissioners; and once in four years, in addition to these, a Probate Judge, and *Electors* of President and Vice-President of the United States. The State is divided into nine districts, for the election of Representatives in Congress.

On the first Monday in April, of each year, in each organized township, the people elect a Supervisor, a Justice of the Peace, a Township Clerk, a Commissioner of Highways, a Township Treasurer, a School Inspector, not exceeding four

Constables, and one Overseer of Highways for each highway district.

Judges of the Supreme and Circuit Courts, Regents of the State University, and County Superintendents of Schools, are also elected at the April elections.

In addition to these, elections are held in cities and villages, of officers to discharge the duties required of them under the charter and by-laws of such city or village.

Questions—In treating of the officers required to carry on the government, under what general *classification* do we refer to them? At what time is the general election for the State and county officers held? Name the officers elected at the general election. Into how many districts is the State divided for the election of Representatives in Congress? At what time are township officers elected? Name the township officers. What other officers are elected at the spring election?

CHAPTER XVII.

QUALIFICATIONS OF ELECTORS — NATURALIZATION OF FOR-
EIGNERS.

The right to vote is called the right of suffrage.

Persons who have the right to make choice of public officers, and to vote, are called electors.

In all elections, every male citizen, every male inhabitant residing in the State, on the twenty-fourth day of June, 1835; every male inhabitant residing in the State, on the first day of January, 1850, who has declared his intention to become a citizen of the United States, pursuant to the laws thereof, six months *preceding* an election, or who has resided in the State two years and six months, and declared his intention as *afore-*

said, and every *civilized* male *inhabitant* of Indian *descent*, a *native* of the United States and not a member of any *tribe*, shall be an elector and entitled to vote; but no citizen or inhabitant shall be an elector or entitled to vote at any election unless he shall be above the age of twenty-one years, and have resided in this State three months, and in the township or ward in which he offers to vote ten days next preceding such election. *Provided*, that in time of war, insurrection, or rebellion, no qualified elector in the actual military service of the United States, or of this State, in the army or navy thereof, shall be deprived of his vote by reason of his absence from the township, ward, or State in which he resides; and the Legislature shall have the power, and shall provide the manner in which, and the time and place at which, such absent electors may vote, and for the canvass and return of their votes to the township or ward election district in which they respectively reside, or otherwise.

Persons born in other countries are called *aliens;* and to become citizens must be naturalized. To accomplish this, the person desiring to become a citizen must go before the Court or the clerk thereof, two years before he can be admitted as a citizen, and declare, on oath, in writing, that he intends to become a citizen of the United States, and to *renounce* his *allegiance* to his former government; and he must declare on oath that he will support the Constitution of the United States. Then, two years thereafter, the Court, if satisfied as to his *moral character* and loyalty, and that he has resided in the United States for five years, and in the State or Territory where the Court is held, for one year, may admit him as a citizen.

Persons residing within and under the jurisdiction of the United States, at any time between the 18th of June, 1778, and April 14, 1802, and who have continued to reside therein, are exempt from the provisions of the preceding paragraph.

Any alien being a minor, who arrives in the United States when not over eighteen years of age, and continues to reside therein, may, after he arrives at the age of twenty-one years, and after he shall have resided five years within the United States, be admitted as a citizen, without having made the usual declaration three years previous to his admission; but this declaration must be made at the time of his admission, and he must declare to the Court on oath, and prove that for three years next preceding, it has been his intention to become a citizen of the United States.

When an alien, who shall have complied with the provisions of paragraph four, of this chapter, relative to declaring his intention, may die before being naturalized, his widow and children shall be considered citizens of the United States, and entitled to all the privileges as such, upon taking the oath prescribed by law.

Aliens having borne any *hereditary* title, or been of any of the orders of nobility in the Kingdom or State from which they came, must *renounce* such title, or order of nobility, before they can be admitted as citizens of the United States.

When at war with other nations, the United States Government will not admit to citizenship, the citizens, subjects, or denizens of such nation.

As to the provisions of law concerning aliens residing in the United States prior to 1812, the student is referred to the abstract of the laws of the United States, to be found at page 2245, of the Compiled Laws of Michigan.

The children of naturalized persons, being under the age of twenty-one years at the time of their parents being naturalized, shall, if dwelling in the United States, be considered as citizens thereof.

Children of persons who are or have been citizens of the United States, though born elsewhere, are considered as citizens of the United States.

Any alien, of the age of twenty-one years and upwards, who has enlisted or shall enlist in the armies of the United States, either the regular or the volunteer forces, and has been, or shall be hereafter, honorably discharged, may be admitted to become a citizen of the United States, upon his petition, without any previous declaration of his intention to become a citizen of the United States ; and he shall not be required to prove more than one year's residence within the United States previous to his application to become such citizen; and the Court admitting such alien, shall, in addition to such proof of residence and good moral character, as is now provided by law, be satisfied, by competent proof, of such person having been honorably discharged from the service of the United States as aforesaid.

Aliens may be admitted to citizenship by any Court of Record having *common-law jurisdiction*, and a seal, or clerk or *prothonotary*.

Questions — What is the right to vote called? Who are called electors? Who are electors in Michigan? What is an alien? How are aliens naturalized? What is said of residents of the United States between June 18th, 1778, and April 14th, 1802? Of alien minors who arrive in this country while under the age of eighteen years? Of the widow and children of aliens who die before being fully admitted to citizenship? Of aliens having hereditary titles, or belonging to orders of nobility? When will certain aliens not be admitted? What is said of the minor children of naturalized persons? Of children of American citizens, born in other countries? What is said of the naturalization of persons who have enlisted in the military service of the United States, and been honorably discharged? In what Courts may aliens be admitted to citizenship?

CHAPTER XVIII.

ELECTIONS — HOW CONDUCTED — CHALLENGE OF PERSONS: OFFERING TO VOTE.

At the general election, the Supervisor, the Justice of the Peace whose term of office will first expire, and the Township Clerk of each township, and the Assessor and Alderman of each ward in a city, or if in any city there be not an Assessor in every ward, then the two Aldermen of each ward, shall be the inspectors of election. These officers constitute a Board.

The Township Clerk, assisted by some other person, acts as clerk of the election. He provides a box with an opening in the lid, through which each ballot received must be *inserted*, and keeps two *lists* of the names of all persons voting at the election. The ballot consists of a paper ticket on which is written or printed the names of the persons for whom the voter intends to vote, and the offices to which the persons named on the ballot are intended to be chosen. The person offering to vote delivers his ballot to one of the inspectors, in the presence of the Board.

The inspectors or any elector qualified to vote at the election, may challenge any person offering to vote; that is, may object to such person voting, on the ground that he has not the legal qualifications entitling him to vote. When such a challenge is made, one of the inspectors administers an oath or affirmation to the person challenged, and if such person shall swear or affirm that he is qualified, his vote must be received. The form of the oath, or affirmation, must be such as to contain the grounds of the voter's qualification. Thus, if he is a citizen of the United States, is twenty-one years of age, and has resided in the State and township or ward during the time required by law, the form of the oath is:

"You do solemnly swear [or affirm] that you are twenty-one years of age; that you are a citizen of the United States; that you have resided in this State three months next preceding this day, and in the township (or ward, as the case may be) ten days next preceding this day, and that you have not voted at this election."

Questions—What officers constitute the inspectors of election? Who acts as clerk of the election? What is the clerk required to provide and to do in relation to the election? What is a ballot? In what way do electors vote? What is meant by challenging a person who offers to vote? In what way do the inspectors determine whether a person challenged is qualified to vote?

CHAPTER XIX.

OF ELECTIONS, CONTINUED — CANVASS OF VOTES AND RETURN OF STATEMENTS.

When the polls are closed, the ballots are examined and a statement of the result is prepared in *duplicate*, and *certified* to by the inspectors. One of these statements is *filed* with the township or city clerk, and the other is delivered to one of the inspectors *designated* by the Board, to attend the county canvass, to be delivered to the county clerk.

The inspectors so designated, from the different towns in the county, meet at the office of the county clerk, on the Tuesday next after the election, and organize themselves into a Board of Canvassers, and proceed to examine the statements sent from the inspectors.

Sometimes a county has more than one Senatorial or Representative district. In such case each district has a Board of Canvassers, so far as the canvass relates to Senators and Representatives, consisting of the inspectors representing the towns in such districts.

The County Canvassers are required to make a separate statement, containing the whole number of votes given in such county for the State officers, and the names of the persons for whom such votes were given, and the number of votes given for each; another, of the votes given for Representative in Congress. Copies of these statements are sent to the Governor, Secretary of State, and State Treasurer; and the result of the canvass for members of the Legislature is certified to, and delivered to the persons elected.

Questions — When the polls are closed, how are the votes canvassed? Who constitute the Board of County Canvassers? What are their duties? State how the votes are canvassed for Senators and Representatives where the district is less than a whole county. To what persons are the results of the canvass sent?

CHAPTER XX.

OF ELECTIONS, CONTINUED — PROCEEDINGS IN CASE OF TIE VOTE — CANVASSERS — CONSTITUTIONAL AMENDMENTS.

In each election district, for the election of a Senator or Representative, or where, in elections for county officers or members of the Legislature, two or more persons receive an equal number of votes for the same office, as many strips of paper as there are such persons, are prepared, and on one of the strips is written the word " Elected," and on the others " Not Elected." These are placed in a box and each of the aforesaid persons draws one of the slips therefrom, and the person drawing the slip on which is the word " Elected," is deemed elected to the office in question.

In each election district, of a Senator or Representative, in the State Legislature, the limits of which are greater than those of a county, there is a Board of District Canvassers, composed of the clerks of the several counties within the district, the Judge of Probate and the Sheriff of the county in which the meetings of the Board are held. The result of their canvass is filed with the clerk of the county where their meeting is held, and such clerk sends a copy thereof to the Secretary of State, and another copy to the person elected.

The Secretary of State, the State Treasurer, and the Commissioner of the State Land Office constitute the Board of State Canvassers. These canvassers determine from the returns sent by the county clerks, who are elected State officers and Representatives in Congress, to whom the Secretary of State sends certificates of election. They also determine who are elected Electors of President and Vice-President.

The Legislature sometimes proposes amendments to the constitution, and submits them to the people, who at the general election vote thereon. The State canvassers determine the vote of the people, on such measures.

Questions—In the election of county officers and members of the Legislature, what course is pursued when two or more persons receive an equal number of votes for the same office? Who compose the board of canvassers, where the limits of the Senatorial and Representative districts are greater than a county? What disposition is made with the statement of the result of the canvass in such cases? What officers constitute the Board of State Canvassers? What are their duties?

4

CHAPTER XXI.

The people do not vote directly for President and Vice-President of the United States, but the voters of each State choose a number of men equal to the number of Senators and Representatives to which it is entitled in Congress. These are called Presidential Electors. The State of Michigan is entitled to two Senators and nine Representatives in Congress. Hence we choose eleven Electors.

These Electors *convene* at the State Capitol, on the first Wednesday in December next after the election, and vote for President and Vice-President, and make a list of the persons voted for, and the number of votes for each, which is sent to the President of the United States Senate.

On the second Wednesday of February, the President of the Senate, in the presence of all the Senators and Representatives, opens all the certificates, and the votes are counted. The persons having a majority of all the Electoral votes for President and Vice-President are declared elected.

In case a person receives a *plurality* of the Electoral votes for President, but not a majority, the House of Representatives elects a President.

Suppose there are three candidates for the office, and that of the 359 electoral votes, one candidate should receive 150 votes, another 130 votes, and the other 79. Now, a majority of 359 cannot be less than 180 ; consequently neither would be elected. In such case the House of Representatives would elect a President, the members of each State voting by themselves, and the candidate receiving a majority of the Representatives of a State, has one vote for such majority ; that is, there are as many Presidential votes as there are States, and the person who receives the votes of a majority of the States is elected.

If the Electors fail to elect a Vice-President, the Senate, in a body, chooses one from the two having the highest number of Electoral votes.

Questions — How do people vote for President and Vice-President of the United States? To how many Presidential Electors is the State of Michigan entitled? What is done with the statement of the vote of the electors? When and where is the vote of the various States counted and the result declared? In case no person receives a majority of all the votes cast for President, how is the President elected? What is the difference between a plurality and a majority? In case the Electors fail to elect a Vice-President, how is that officer elected?

CHAPTER XXII.

OF THE LEGISLATIVE DEPARTMENT — ITS POWERS AND DUTIES.

We have already seen how Senators and Representatives in the State Legislature are elected.

The Legislative power is vested in a Senate and House of Representatives.

Senators and Representatives must be citizens of the United States, and qualified electors in the respective Counties and Districts which they represent.

The Legislature meets every two years, at the State

Capitol at Lansing, on the first Wednesday in January. The room in which the Senators meet is called the Senate Chamber, and the room in which the Representatives meet is called the Representative Hall, or Hall of Representatives.

Every Senator and every Representative takes an *oath* to support the Constitution of the United States, and the Constitution of the State of Michigan, and that he will faithfully discharge the duties of his office, according to the best of his ability.

A majority of each House constitutes a *quorum*. Each House determines the rules of its proceedings, and judges of the qualifications, election, and returns of its members. Each House keeps a journal of its proceedings, and publishes the same, except such parts as may require secrecy. The yeas and nays, that is, the way in which members vote on any question, must be entered on the journal, at the request of one-fifth of the members elected. The House of Representatives chooses one of its members to preside over it, who is called a Speaker. The Lieutenant-Governor is the presiding officer in the Senate, and is called a President.

The presiding officer preserves order, and sees that the business of the House is properly attended to. When a question is to be decided, the presiding officer "puts it to vote;" that is, requests the members to express their judgment in favor of or against the measure. Those who favor the measure, say "*aye;*" those who oppose it, say "*no.*"

The officers of the Senate consist of a President, Secretary, Assistant Secretary, Sergeant-at-Arms, Assistant Sergeant-at-Arms, Engrossing and Enrolling Clerk, Assistant Engrossing and Enrolling Clerk, Janitors, Clerks of Committees, and Messengers.

The officers of the House of Representatives consist of a Speaker, Clerk, Corresponding Clerk, Journal Clerk, Engrossing and Enrolling Clerk, Assistant Engrossing and Enrolling Clerk, Clerks of Committees, Sergeant-at-Arms, Assistant Sergeant-at-Arms, and Messengers. A Postmaster, Firemen, Assistant Firemen, and Keepers of the Cloak Room, are employed by both Houses.

Questions — In what bodies is the Legislative power vested? What are the qualifications of members of the Legislature? At what times does the Legislature meet? Name the Rooms in which the two Houses meet. What oath do members take? What body fixes the rules governing the Legislature, and determines the qualifications of its members? What record is kept by the Legislature? What officers preside over the Legislature? What are the duties of the presiding officers? Name the officers of the Senate. Name the officers of the House.

CHAPTER XXIII.

OF THE ENACTMENT OF LAWS — ELECTION OF UNITED STATES SENATORS.

When the two Houses are organized and ready for business, the Governor presents to them his message. This is a written statement of the condition of the State, and calls attention to such subjects as the Governor thinks need legislation.

The presiding officers of the respective Houses usually appoint committees, to whom are referred the different subjects presented for the consideration of the Legislature. Sometimes, however, committees are elected by the House or Senate, instead of being appointed by the presiding officer. These committees consider and report upon the matters referred to them. In the Senate there are now thirty-nine of these committees, and in the House, forty.

Were it not for these committees it would be almost impossible to transact all the business presented to the Legislature. Some measures are presented by the Governor and others by the members. The people sometimes want a law passed, and procure a paper to be drawn up, containing their wishes, which is called a petition, and send it to the Legislature. Now suppose this petition asks the Legislature to pass a law in regard to education; the petition is referred to the Committee on Education. If the petition relates to insurance, it is referred to the Committee on Insurance, and so on. Sometimes members or others, draw up bills which they desire to have passed by the Legislature. A bill is a draft of a proposed law; or it may be defined as "an instrument presented to a legislative body for its approbation, and enactment." These bills are referred to the appropriate committees. If the bills so referred are considered proper and necessary, the committee report in favor of them and recommend that they be passed — that is, enacted into a law.

These committees frequently draft bills and report them to the House. If a committee reports against a measure referred to them, the House generally concurs with their recommendation and dismisses the subject.

If a member of either house desires the passage of a law, he gives notice that on some future day he will ask leave to introduce a bill for that purpose. But in all cases, at least one day's notice must be given of his intention to ask such leave.

It is not deemed necessary to state here all the particular forms through which a bill must pass before it can become a law. It is perhaps sufficient to say that, after it has been discussed and amended, a final vote is taken on the question:

"Shall the bill pass?" If a majority of the members vote "aye," it is passed; if not, it is lost.

When a bill is passed by one house, it is sent to the other, when it is duly considered and voted upon. If it passes that house, without amendment, it is sent to the Governor for his approval; and if he approves it he attaches his *signature* and it becomes a law.

If a bill is amended in the second house, it is sent back to the house where it originated; and when both houses finally agree, the bill is sent to the Governor.

If the Governor does not approve the bill, he declines to sign it, and returns it with his reasons for withholding his approval, to the house where it originated. This act of the Governor is called his *veto*, which is a Latin word, meaning, *I forbid*. Notwithstanding the veto, if two-thirds of the members of both houses shall, thereafter, approve the bill, it becomes a law.

If any bill be not returned by the Governor within ten days, Sundays excepted, after it has been presented to him, it becomes a law, as if he had signed it, unless the Legislature, by their adjournment, prevent its return; in which case it does not become a law.

The Governor may approve, sign, and file in the office of the Secretary of State, within five days after the adjournment of the Legislature, any act passed during the last five days of the session; and the same thereupon becomes a law.

The Legislature elect United States Senators. Each State is entitled to two Senators, who are elected for the term of six years.

Questions— When the two houses of the Legislature are organized, what duty does the Governor perform? What is said of the appointment of committees? How many committees has the Senate? How many committees has the House of Representatives? What are the duties of these committees? What is a bill? When a bill is introduced, what course is usually pursued with reference to it? In case a member wishes to introduce a bill, what does he do? When a bill is passed in one house, what is done with it? How can a bill become a law when the Governor refuses to approve it? State what becomes of a bill if not returned by the Governor within ten days from the time it is presented to him. In case of an adjournment before all the bills passed have been returned by the Governor, how may they become effectual as laws? What members of Congress do the Legislature elect?

CHAPTER XXIV.

EXECUTIVE DEPARTMENT — DUTIES OF THE GOVERNOR AND OTHER OFFICERS.

The Executive department is vested in the Governor, who, in the discharge of his duties, is assisted by a number of *subordinate* officers.

A person to be *eligible* to the office of Governor or Lieutenant-Governor, must have been a citizen of the United States for at least five years, and a resident of this State two years next preceding his election, and must be thirty years of age or upwards.

The Governor and Lieutenant-Governor are elected for two years.

The Governor is Commander-in-Chief of the military and naval forces of the State, and may call out such forces to execute the laws, to suppress insurrections, and to repel invasions. He transacts all necessary business for the State with the officers of the government. He may convene the Legislature on *extraordinary* occasions.

He informs the Legislature of such measures as he deems *expedient.*

He may grant reprieves, commutations, and pardons for all offenses except *treason* and cases of *impeachment.* If a person has been found guilty of an offense and is sentenced to be punished, the Governor has power to postpone or put off the time when the punishment shall commence. This is called a *reprieve.* If he should set the person free and discharge him from punishment, this would be called a *pardon.*

By *commutation* is meant the change of a punishment to which a person has been condemned, into a less severe one.

The Lieutenant-Governor is, by virtue of his office, President of the Senate, and in case of the impeachment of the Governor, his removal from office, death, inability, resignation, or absence from the State, the duties of the office devolve upon the Lieutenant-Governor.

The Secretary of State is an executive officer. It is his duty to countersign all commissions issued by the Governor. The original acts of the Legislature are deposited with him. He is to furnish laws for publication; to distribute the statutes; to give notice of vacancies to be filled at a general election; to record statements of votes transmitted by County Clerks, and the statement of State Canvassers; to issue certificates of election to United States Senators; to record deeds and other evidences of title in the State; to *countersign* State bonds and certificates, and to discharge many other duties prescribed by law.

Questions—In whom is the executive department vested? What are the qualifications for Governor? For how long a term are Governor and Lieutenant-Governor elected? What is the Governor's relation to the military and naval forces of the State? Enumerate other powers and duties of the Governor. What is a Reprieve? Pardon? Commutation? What are some of the duties of Lieutenant-Governor? Mention some of the duties of Secretary of State.

CHAPTER XXV.

OF STATE OFFICERS AND THEIR DUTIES, CONTINUED — AUDITOR-GENERAL — STATE TREASURER — COMMISSIONER OF THE LAND OFFICE — SUPERINTENDENT OF PUBLIC INSTRUCTION — ATTORNEY-GENERAL.

The Auditor-General may be called an executive officer. Among the many duties he is required to perform, the following may be mentioned: He is to state accounts and liquidate claims against the State; to adjust claims in favor of the State; to keep accounts between the Treasurer and the State; to report to the Legislature upon the funds of the State; to estimate and charge *specific tax* on corporations, and to issue warrants for the collection thereof; to apportion the State tax, and to make out and transmit to the clerks of Boards of Supervisors statements of amounts apportioned to counties.

The State Treasurer has charge of the public moneys that are paid into the State Treasury. It is his duty to make a report to the Legislature, embracing a statement of the balance in the Treasury to the credit of the State, with a summary of the receipts and payments made by the Treasury.

The Commissioner of the State Land Office has the general charge of all lands belonging to the State, or in which it has an interest; and he is authorized to lease, sell, and dispose of the same in the manner prescribed by law.

The Superintendent of Public Instruction has the general

supervision of public instruction in the State, and of the State Reform School. It is his duty to *transmit* to the Governor, to be by him transmitted to the Legislature, a report containing,

First.—A statement of the condition of the University and of all incorporated literary institutions and primary schools.

Second.—Estimates and amounts of expenditures of the school moneys.

Third.—Plans for the improvement and management of all educational funds, and for the better organization of the educational system, if, in his opinion, the same be required.

Fourth.—The condition of the Normal School.

Fifth.—The annual reports and accompanying documents, as far as he shall deem the same of sufficient public interest, of the Board of Control of the State Reform School.

He is required to publish the school laws, and to furnish necessary forms for conducting proceedings under such laws; to apportion the school fund, and to do many other acts provided for by law.

The Attorney-General is the law-officer of the State. The following are some of his duties :

He is to prosecute and defend for the State, in actions in the Supreme Court, and in other courts, when directed so to do by the Governor or the Legislature; to prosecute and defend suits on request of State officers; to consult with and advise Prosecuting Attorneys; to appear for the State before State Auditors.

Questions—Mention some of the duties of the Auditor-General. Of the Commissioner of the State Land Office. Of Superintendent of Public Instruction. Of the Attorney-General.

CHAPTER XXVI.

OF STATE BOARDS AND COMMISSIONERS.

The word *Board* is used to designate a body of persons whose duty it is to manage or control some institution, or to discharge certain specific duties.

Provision has been made by law for the establishment of various Boards, to discharge duties in which the people of the whole State are more or less interested.

It is frequently the case that for the discharge of particular duties, a single person is employed, called a Commissioner. If two or more are employed, we refer to them as a Board, or Board of Commissioners. Some of these Commissioners are appointed by the Governor, others are elected by the people, while some of them are designated by name, in the law creating the office and prescribing the duties thereof.

The various State Boards are, with few exceptions, composed of State officers, who, in addition to their other duties, are required by law to act together in managing and controling certain public interests. Some of these Boards are appointed by the Governor. Among the various Boards provided for by law, we may mention the Board of Agriculture, which has charge of the Agricultural College and its interests; the Board of Canvassers, established to examine the statements of votes received by the Secretary of State, for State officers, Representatives in Congress, and Presidential Electors; the Board of Control for the Reform School for *juvenile* offenders; the Board of Control, to have the charge of the canals in the Upper Peninsula; the Board to take charge of lands given to the State by Congress, for railroads; the Board to have the charge of the State Public School at Coldwater; the Board of Education, to have charge of the State Normal School; the Board of Equalization, to see that the money or tax to be raised for State purposes is fairly and *equitably levied* throughout the State; the Board of Regents, who are elected by the people, and who have charge of the State University; the Board of State Auditors, whose duty it is to examine and *adjust* claims against the State; the Board of *Escheats*, to take charge of the property, for the State, of those who die without a will and without *heirs;* the State Military Board, to audit claims of a military character; the Boards having control of our Asylums.

Among the many Commissioners employed to discharge public duties in this State, we may mention Commissioners to make settlement, on the division of counties; to examine securities of insurance companies, and to see that they comply with the provisions of law; to procure information and statistics relative to the scientific treatment and cure of the victims of intemperance; to see that railroad companies comply with the laws, rules, and regulations established for their management.

For the benefit of those who desire a more particular statement, concerning the various State Boards and their duties, a note is appended to this chapter.

Questions—What is meant by the word *Board*, as used in this lesson? For what purposes are Boards established? Who generally constitute the State Boards? Mention some of the State Boards and their duties. Mention some of the Commissioners and their duties.

NOTE.—The State Board of Agriculture consists of six members, besides the Governor of the State, and the President of the State Agricultural College, who are by virtue of their office, members of the Board. The members of this Board are appointed by the Governor. They meet quarterly at the State Agricultural College at Lansing; they have the general control of the Agricultural College, the farm pertaining thereto, and of the lands belonging to the College, and of all appropriations made therefor. The Secretary of the Board is paid a salary of one thousand dollars per annum. He is required to keep a record of the transactions of the Board; to encourage such domestic industry and household arts as are calculated to promote the general thrift, wealth, and resources of the State; the formation of agricultural societies, the *importation* of improved breeds of horses, cattle, sheep, hogs, and other animals, and to procure and distribute seeds, plants. trees, and shrubbery.

The Secretary of State, the State Treasurer and Commissioner of the State Land Office, constitute a Board of State Canvassers. It is the duty of this Board to examine the statements received by the Secretary of State, of the votes given in the several counties, and make a statement of the votes given for the State officers, Representatives in Congress, Presidential Electors, and the votes given for constitutional amendments, and in relation to banking laws.

The Governor, Secretary of State, Auditor-General, Treasurer, Attorney-General, and Commissioner of the State Land Office, constitute a Board of Control for the reclamation of swamp lands by means of State roads and ditches. The Legislature having made provision for the drainage of certain swamp lands belonging to the State, by the construction of roads with proper ditches and drains, at the expense of the State, the Board of Control was organized to direct and control such work.

Board of Control for the Reform School.—A House of Correction, known as the Reform School, for the correction of offenders under sixteen years of age, is located at Lansing. This institution is under the control and supervision of a Board consisting of three persons appointed by the Governor.

About twenty years ago (1854–5), a ship-canal was constructed at Sault Ste. Marie. to *facilitate* the passage of vessels going to and returning from Lake Superior. This canal is under State control, and a Board, consisting of the Governor, State Treasurer, and Auditor-General, has been created by law, to have charge of this public improvement. The Governor appoints a Superintendent who has the immediate charge of the canal, and who collects tolls from vessels passing through it.

On the third day of June, 1856, Congress granted to this State a large quantity of lands for railroad purposes. A Board to manage and dispose of all lands appropriated for the construction of railroads, and to do any and all other acts necessary and proper respecting the construction of said railroads. which may be prescribed by law. consisting of the Governor and six Commissioners appointed by him, has been provided for.

In 1871. the Legislature provided for the establishment of a School for dependent and neglected children. This school has been established at Coldwater, and is under the management of a Board, consisting of three persons appointed by the Governor, called a Board of Control of the State Public School.

A State Normal School has been established at Ypsilanti, for the instruction of persons. both male and female, in the art of teaching. Also to give instruction in the mechanical arts. and in the arts of husbandry and agricultural chemistry; in the fundamental laws of the United States. and with regard to the rights and duties of citizens. This school is under the control of a Board of Education, consisting of three persons, elected by the people, in addition to the Superintendent of Public Instruction, who is a member and Secretary of the Board.

State Board of Equalization. · For the purpose of raising money to support the Government, a levy is made upon all the property of the State, and a certain per cent. of its value is required to be paid. For this purpose the lands and personal property of all the people are appraised, and this appraisal is certified to, and sent to the Auditor-General by the clerks of the different counties. In order that the money or tax to be raised for the State may be levied upon all the property of the State fairly and equitably, a Board of Equalization has been established, consisting of the Lieutenant-Governor, Auditor-General, Secretary of State, State Treasurer, and Commissioner of the Land Office. It is the duty of this Board to examine the statements sent to them, from the different counties, and to determine whether the relative valuation between the several counties is equal and uniform, according to location, soil, improvements, productions and manufactures, and whether the personal estates have been uniformly *estimated*. If they are found to be *relatively* unequal, they equalize them by adding to or deducting from the aggregate valuation of taxable real and personal estate in such county or counties, such percentage as will produce relative equal and uniform valuations between the several counties in the State.

The State Treasurer, Auditor-General, and Secretary of State, constitute the Board of Fund Commissioners. The statute creating this Board, makes it their duty, when there is more money in the treasury than is necessary to pay the current expenses of the State, and the interest on its indebtedness, to pay a portion of the principal indebtedness. A more recent statute, however, confers power upon the Treasurer to make payment upon the indebtedness of the State, whenever he shall have a *surplus* of money.

The Governor, Superintendent of Public Instruction, and the President of the State Board of Education, constitute a Board of Geological Survey. They have control of the geological survey of the State, and for that purpose, may, from time to time, appoint such person or persons to assist in making such survey as may be deemed necessary.

For the management and control of the State University, eight Regents are elected by the people, who have power to enact ordinances, by-laws, and regulations for the government of the University; to elect a president, to fix, increase, and reduce the regular number of professors and tutors, and to appoint the same, and to determine the amount of their salaries, and to do such other business as may be necessary for the management and control of the University.

The Board of Commissioners for the general supervision of penal, pauper, and reformatory institutions, consists of three members appointed by the Governor. It is their duty to visit the city and county poor-houses, county jails, Reform School, State Prison, Detroit House of Correction, State and County Asylums for the insane, and the deaf, dumb, and blind, to ascertain the condition of such institutions, and how they are conducted and managed. They are to report to the Governor the result of their investigations. They are also to report to the Governor such changes in the penal and criminal laws and the laws concerning these institutions. as they think are proper. The Governor may appoint one or more females to visit the institutions above referred to, and investigate the treatment and provision made for women and children.

The Secretary of State, State Treasurer, and Commissioner of the State Land Office, constitute the Board of State Auditors. It is their duty to examine and adjust all claims against the State, not otherwise provided for by general law.

The Board of State Swamp Land Road Commissioners consists of two members, appointed by the Governor. These Commissioners superintend the letting of all contracts upon State swamp land roads, or reject contracts made by the local commissioners. They are to inspect the work of contractors on the swamp roads; to examine into all trespasses on swamp lands of the State, and to prosecute therefor and collect damages for such trespasses. The Board of Commissioners are to report to the Board of Control, and in some respects are subordinate to them.

Whenever any person dies without having made a *will*, and without any legal heirs, the property of such person is *escheated* to the State. *Escheat* means a thing fallen to. Thus, when there is no relative to take the property of one who dies, his property falls to the State, or is *escheated* to the State. The Auditor-General, State Treasurer, and Secretary of State, constitute a Board of Trustees to take charge and dispose of, for the State, all such property.

The Superintendent of Public Instruction appoints, every two years, two persons as a Board of Visitors, whose duty it is to make personal examination into the state and condition of the University in all its departments and branches, at least once in each year, and to report the result to the Superintendent, suggesting such improvements as they may deem important.

The Board of Education appoint a similar Board, consisting of three persons, to examine into the affairs of the Normal School, and to report to the Superintendent.

A ship-canal has been constructed across Keweenaw Point, in the Upper Peninsula, from Portage Lake to Lake Superior, known as the Portage Lake and Lake Superior Ship Canal, and by law, the Governor, Auditor-General, and State Treasurer, are constituted a Board of Control to establish and regulate tolls on the canal, and to make suitable rules and regulations regarding the care and improvement of the same, and to appoint a Superintendent to have charge of it.

The Board of Fish Commissioners consists of two persons appointed by the Governor. It is the duty of the Board to supervise generally the fishing interests, and secure the enforcement of all laws relating to the protection of fish and *fisheries* in the State. They are to establish a State fish-breeding establishment, for the *artificial propagation* and *cultivation* of fish; and to appoint a Superintendent to take charge of the raising of fish at the fishery.

The State Military Board consists of the Inspector-General and two persons appointed by the Governor, who hold their office for two years. The Board is an advisory body to the Commander-in-Chief. It is their duty to audit all claims of a military character against the State, and to make rules and regulations for the government of the State troops.

The Board of Trustees of the Michigan Asylum for the Insane, and also the Board of Trustees of the Michigan Asylum for the Deaf, Dumb, and Blind, consists of three persons each appointed by the Governor. These institutions and the property thereof, are under the control of these Trustees.

CHAPTER XXVII.

OF COUNTIES AND COUNTY OFFICERS.

As it would be impossible for the State officers whose duties we have considered, to transact all the public business necessary for the people, the State has been subdivided into smaller portions of territory, each of which has a government, not inconsistent with that of the State. Of these subdivisions, the largest, for the purposes of government, are counties. The counties usually embrace about sixteen townships each.

Most of the county officers are elected by the people, and consist of a Probate Judge, Sheriff, Clerk, Treasurer, Register of Deeds, Prosecuting Attorney, County Surveyor, two Coroners, Superintendent of Schools, and Circuit Court Commissioners. In some of the larger counties, two Circuit Court Commissioners are elected. Three Superintendents of the Poor are elected by the Board of Supervisors. There may be elected in each county, inspectors of beef and pork, butter and lard, fish, flour and meal, leather, and pot and pearl ashes.

A Board of Supervisors is established in each county, consisting of one member from each township, and where there are cities within the county, such cities are entitled to as many Supervisors as may be prescribed by the Legislature.

The Probate Judge and Inspectors hold their offices for four years; Superintendents of the Poor, for three years; and other county officers for two years. Supervisors, who are properly township officers, hold their office for one year. In the county of Wayne there is a Board of Auditors, consisting of three persons, who hold their office for three years.

5

Each county has a county-seat; that is, a place where the public business of the county is transacted. A court-house, a jail, and fire-proof offices are necessary at the county-seat.

Supervisors are elected at the annual township meeting in April, in each township, and at the Spring election in cities. These Supervisors, in addition to the duties they perform in their respective townships and cities, constitute a Board to transact business in which all the people of the county are interested. They accordingly meet at the court-house, at the county-seat, on the second Monday of October, in each year, and at such other times as may be necessary. They have power to purchase land for the use of the county, or to authorize the sale of lands belonging to the county; to cause to be built necessary buildings for the use of the county; to borrow money, or raise by tax money for the use of the county in making improvements authorized by law; to prescribe and fix the compensation for all services rendered for, and adjust all claims against their respective counties; to provide for the raising of money to defray the current expenses of the county; to make such laws and regulations as they may deem necessary for the destruction of wild beasts, of thistles and other noxious weeds, within their counties; to authorize townships to borrow or raise by tax any sum of money, not exceeding one thousand dollars, in any township, in any one year, to build or repair any roads or bridges in such township or townships; to divide their county into representative districts equal to the number of representatives to which such county is by law entitled; to divide or alter in its bounds any township, and to erect new townships; to equalize and correct the assessment for taxes; to *apportion* the state and county taxes between the several townships, and to do many other things prescribed by law.

The Board of County Auditors of Wayne County have

all the powers of Boards of Supervisors in the other counties, except in relation to taxes.

Questions — What are the largest subdivisions of the State, for the purposes of government? How many townships are usually embraced in a county? Name the county officers. What board is established in each county? For what length of time are county officers elected? In addition to the Board of Supervisors, what board is established in the county of Wayne? What do we call the place where the public business of the county is transacted? What public buildings are required at the county-seat? At what times do the Board of Supervisors meet? Mention some of their powers and duties. What powers have the Board of County Auditors of Wayne County?

CHAPTER XXVIII.

OF COUNTY OFFICERS — COUNTY TREASURER — JUDGE OF PROBATE — PROSECUTING ATTORNEY — COUNTY CLERK — SHERIFFS.

It is the duty of the County Treasurer to receive all moneys belonging to the county; and to pay the same out in the manner provided by law. Some of the money received by him belongs to the State; this he pays over to the State Treasurer. Some of it is paid out to the county officers for their salary, and some of it to the officers and jurors who attend the courts. The moneys received by him for the use of the county, he pays out on the orders of the Board of Supervisors.

The Judge of Probate holds his court at the county-seat. His duties will be noticed when considering the Judicial Department.

It is the duty of the Prosecuting Attorney to prosecute

or defend all suits in the county, in which the State or county is a party. It is his duty to prosecute those who commit crimes within his county; to give opinions, where the State or county may be a party in interest, when required so to do by any of the civil officers in the discharge of their duties, relating to the interest of the State or county. The Board of Supervisors fix the salary of the Prosecuting Attorney.

The County Clerk is, by virtue of his office, clerk of the Circuit Court, and keeps the records of papers *pertaining* to that Court. He is also clerk of the Board of Supervisors and of the County and District Canvassers. In addition to many other duties, he is required to keep a record of all the births, deaths, and marriages in his county. Articles of association of the different corporations within his county, and certificates of the formation of religious societies, are filed in his office and recorded by him. His salary is fixed by the Board of Supervisors, but in addition to this he receives fees fixed by law, for the discharge of most of the duties performed by him.

The Sheriff has the charge and custody of the jails in his county; and of the prisoners of the same. Of the many duties he has to perform, we may mention his duty to execute and serve writs and orders directed to him by the courts; to attend the Circuit Court and preserve order therein; and to keep the public peace. The Sheriff appoints an Under-Sheriff and deputies to assist him in the discharge of his duties. His fees are fixed by law.

Questions—What are the duties of the County Treasurer? Where does the Judge of Probate hold his office? What are the duties of the Prosecuting Attorney? By whom is his salary fixed? What are the duties of the County Clerk? What are the duties of Sheriff?

CHAPTER XXIX.

OF COUNTY OFFICERS, CONTINUED — CORONERS — REGISTER OF DEEDS — COUNTY SURVEYORS — COUNTY SUPERINTENDENT OF SCHOOLS.

It is the duty of a Coroner, when informed that a person has died suddenly, or from violence, to procure six men to act as jurors, and with them he is to investigate and inquire into the cause and circumstances of the death. This investigation is called a *coroner's inquest*.

Coroners are required by law to discharge the duties of sheriff, when the sheriff is a party interested. Their fees are fixed by law.

The Register of Deeds provides, at the expense of the county, suitable blank books, which he keeps in his office at the county-seat, and in which he copies or records all the deeds, mortgages, and other papers which by law it is proper to record in his office, that may be presented to him.

The object of recording these documents is that they may be preserved, and to give notice to all persons interested, of their existence. The Register of Deeds is paid for recording, by the hundred words.

It is the duty of County Surveyors to make and execute any surveys within their counties that may be required by any court or by any person. These surveys are made to determine the location and boundary lines of lands, and when completed are entered in a record kept by the Surveyor for that purpose.

It is the duty of the County Superintendent of Schools to examine all persons offering themselves as teachers for the public schools. He is required to grant certificates in such form as shall be prescribed by the Superintendent of Public Instruction, licensing as teachers all persons whom he shall deem qualified.

The law provides that it shall be the duty of the County Superintendent,

First.—To visit each of the schools in his county, at least once in each year; to examine carefully into the *discipline* and the *modes* of instruction, and into the progress and *proficiency*, of the pupils, and to make a record of the same; and to counsel with the teachers and district boards as to the course of studies to be pursued; and for the improvement of the instruction and discipline of the school.

Second.—To note the condition of the school-houses and appurtenances thereto, and suggest plans for new school-houses to be erected, and for warming and ventilating the same, and the general improvement of school-houses and grounds.

Third.—To inquire into the condition of district and township libraries, and to counsel, if necessary, for the better management of the same, and to see that the money collected from fines is devoted to the increase of such libraries.

Fourth.—To promote by public lectures and teachers' institutes, and by such other means as he may devise, the improvement of the schools in his county, and the elevation of the character and qualifications of the teachers thereof.

Fifth.—To counsel with teachers and school boards to secure the more general and regular attendance of the children in his county upon the public schools.

The salary of the Superintendent is fixed by the Board of Supervisors.

Questions—What are the duties of Coroners? Of Register of Deeds? Of Surveyors? For what purpose are surveys made? What are the duties of County Superintendent of Schools in relation to teachers? State his other duties as prescribed by law.

CHAPTER XXX.

OF COUNTY OFFICERS, CONTINUED — CIRCUIT COURT COMMIS-
SIONERS — SUPERINTENDENTS OF COUNTY POOR — NOTA-
RIES PUBLIC — INSPECTORS OF PROVISIONS AND OTHER
MERCHANDISE.

Circuit Court Commissioners are authorized to do many
acts which, were it not for their assistance, the Judges would
be required to do. It is frequently necessary, when the
Courts are not in session, that orders should be made and
duties performed affecting the interests of parties whose rights
are to be determined by the Courts. These duties may be
discharged by Circuit Court Commissioners. Testimony to
be used before the Court in Chancery may be taken by a Circuit Court Commissioner; and he may perform many other
duties prescribed by law.

It is the duty of the Superintendents of the County Poor
to take charge of and provide for the wants of those who are
unable to support themselves, and have no relatives able to
support them. They have the control of the poor-houses
erected by the county, for the use of the poor.

Notaries Public are appointed by the Governor, by and
with the consent of the Senate. They are authorized to take
the proof and acknowledgment of deeds; to administer oaths;
to take affidavits; to demand acceptance of bills of exchange
and of promissory notes, and to *protest* the same for non-
acceptance or non-payment.

Inspectors of provisions and other merchandise are required to examine and inspect the provisions and merchandise

of those who keep and offer the same for sale, and to affix a brand or mark to such articles, indicating their quality, so that purchasers may be advised as to what they purchase. Thus, beef is divided into three sorts, " mess," " prime," and " cargo;" and pork into four sorts, " mess pork," " prime pork," " one-hog pork," and " cargo pork."

When provisions or merchandise have been inspected and branded, it is deemed an offense to sell or offer for sale, under such brands, articles different from what such brands indicate.

Questions—What are the duties of Circuit Court Commissioners? Of Superintendents of the County Poor? How are Notaries Public appointed, and what are their duties? What are the duties of Inspectors of provisions and other merchandise? Into how many grades is beef sorted? Into how many grades is pork sorted?

CHAPTER XXXI.

OF TOWNSHIPS AND TOWNSHIP OFFICERS — SUPERVISOR — TOWN-SHIP CLERK — TOWNSHIP BOARD — TOWNSHIP TREASURER —CONSTABLES.

Each organized township has a government of its own, and its people elect officers to administer such government—to discharge certain duties for the good of all the people.

The voters of a township may meet together and make such orders and by-laws for directing and managing the affairs of the township, as they shall deem most conducive to the peace, welfare and good order of the people.

They may annex to such orders and by-laws suitable penalties, not exceeding ten dollars for any breach thereof.

The law provides for the holding of annual meetings in

each township, on the first Monday in April in each year, at which there is elected the following officers: One Supervisor; one Township Clerk; one Treasurer; one School Inspector; two Assessors, if the qualified electors present at the opening of the meeting shall so determine by vote; one Commissioner of Highways; so many Justices of the Peace as there are by law to be elected in the township, and so many Constables as shall be ordered by the meeting, not exceeding four in number, and one Overseer of Highways for each road district, and as many Pound-Masters as the meeting shall direct.

Justices of the Peace hold their terms of office for four years, Highway Commissioners for three years, and School Inspectors for two years. The other officers hold their offices for one year.

The elections at township meetings are held in substantially the same manner as general elections.

The Supervisor is required by law to prosecute for all penalties and forfeitures incurred within his township, and for which no other officer is specially directed to prosecute. He is the Assesssor of his township.

The Township Clerk keeps the records and papers of the township, when no other provision is made by law; he keeps the accounts of the Township with the Treasurer and with each of the several funds belonging to the Township; the minutes of the proceedings of the Township Board, and performs many other duties.

The Supervisor, the two Justices of the Peace whose term of office will soonest expire, and the Township Clerk, constitute the Township Board. It is the duty of this Board to settle all claims against the township.

It is the duty of the Township Treasurer to receive and take charge of all moneys which by law are to be paid into the township treasury.

Constables are ministerial officers of Justices of the Peace. A ministerial officer is one who acts under the authority of a superior, and does what his superior orders him to do.

Constables are also required to serve all warrants, notices and *processes* lawfully directed to them by the Township Board, or the Township Clerk, or any other officer.

Questions — What is said of townships? At what time is the annual township meeting held? What officers are chosen at the annual meeting? For how long a time do the officers hold their offices? How are the elections held? What are some of the duties of the Supervisor? Of the Township Clerk? What officers constitute the Township Board? What are the duties of the Township Treasurer? Of Constables?

CHAPTER XXXII.

OF TOWNSHIP OFFICERS, CONTINUED — COMMISSIONERS OF HIGHWAYS — OVERSEERS OF HIGHWAYS — SCHOOL INSPECTORS — POUND-MASTERS.

Commissioners of Highways have a general supervision and control of all the highways and bridges in their respective townships. They are required to divide their townships into road districts, and to *assign* to each of the districts such of the inhabitants, liable to work on the highways, as shall reside in such district, or own lands therein; to require the Overseers of Highways to have all persons assessed to work on the highways, and perform their labor thereon with such teams, carriages, sleds, or implements as said Commissioners, or any of them, shall direct. It is also their duty to lay out and establish all necessary roads, and to discontinue such old roads as have become unnecessary.

Overseers of Highways are required to repair and keep in order the highways within their districts; to direct persons assessed to work on the highways to come and work; to cause the noxious weeds within the highways to be destroyed, and to execute the orders of the Commissioners.

It is the duty of the School Inspectors to divide the township into school districts; they are to receive from the Treasurer of the township, the money appropriated for the township library, and to procure books for the library. They are also to act in *conjunction* with Inspectors of adjoining townships in the organization of school districts, lying partly in each of said townships.

When *domestic animals* run at large, contrary to law, they may be driven to the township pound; and the keeper of such pound, called a Pound-Master, shall keep them until the owner calls for them, and pays him his fees and the expense of keeping such beasts, and the fees due the person driving them to the pound, for his trouble, and whatever damage they may have done to the person who causes them to be impounded.

Questions — What are the duties of Commissioners of Highways? Of Overseers of Highways? Of School Inspectors? Of Pound-Masters?

CHAPTER XXXIII.

CITIES AND VILLAGES.

A city is a town where a large number of houses and inhabitants are *established* in one place, and which has been *incorporated* and is governed by a *mayor* and *aldermen*.

A village is an assemblage of houses and people, less than a city, and not governed by a Mayor and Aldermen.

There are some villages in Michigan much larger than some of the cities.

Some of these villages are not incorporated ; while others, like cities, find it necessary, for the preservation of good order, and for the purpose of making those public improvements *essential* for the convenience and comfort of the people, to exercise powers of government not conferred upon townships, and therefore such villages become incorporated, and are governed by a President and Trustees.

When we say a town is incorporated, we mean the people of that place have been, by law, united together and authorized to do and perform certain acts which, without such law, they could not do.

The cities, and some villages, have a greater number of officers than the townships. This is necessary for the protection of the people.

Cities are subdivided into *wards* or districts, and officers are elected in each ward to perform certain public duties.

___

Questions—What is a city? A village? Are all the villages incorporated? For what purposes are cities and villages incorporated? What is meant by an incorporated town? What is said of the number of officers? How are cities subdivided?

CHAPTER XXXIV.

OF THE MILITARY DEPARTMENT — STATE TROOPS — GENERAL
OFFICERS — ORGANIZATION OF REGIMENTS — REGIMENTAL
AND COMPANY OFFICERS.

Able-bodied white male citizens, between the ages of
eighteen and forty-five years, are, unless *exempt* by law, subject to military duty.

Ministers of the gospel, judges of the courts, members
and officers of the Legislature ; officers and guards of the
State Prison ; commissioned officers of the militia who have
served six years ; State and county officers, (except notaries
public,) teachers engaged in public institutions and schools ;
keepers of poor-houses ; officers and attendants of the Michigan Asylum for the Insane, in time of peace ; firemen, and
inspectors of provisions and merchandise, except in case of
invasion and *insurrection*, are exempt from military duty.

The officers acting as assessors in the several townships
and cities, on or before the first day of June in each year, are
required to make out and send to the county clerk a list of the
names of persons liable to do military duty. These lists constitute the enrolled militia of the State.

The County Clerk is required to send to the Adjutant-
General of the State the number of persons in his county,
returned to him by the assessors.

In case of war or threatened danger to the State or
United States, from a *foreign* or *domestic* foe, the Commander-
in-Chief (the Governor) may call out any portion or all of the
enrolled militia.

The enrolled militia are not subject to active military duty, except in case of war, *rebellion*, invasion, the prevention of *invasion*, the *suppression* of *riots*, tumults, and breaches of the peace, and to aid civil officers in the execution of the laws and in the service of process.

The active militia are composed of *volunteers* between the ages of eighteen and forty-five years, and are known as State troops, and in case the services of the military are needed, the State troops are first called out; then, if more are needed, a call is made upon the enrolled militia for volunteers, or by *draft*.

The principal military officers provided for by law are, the Commander-in-Chief, one Adjutant-General, one Inspector-General, one Quartermaster-General, one Paymaster-General, and a State Military Board. These officers are appointed by the Governor.

The Adjutant-General distributes orders from the Commander-in-Chief, and attends him when ordered, in the discharge of his duties.

The Inspector-General has charge of the instruction and *mustering* of the State troops.

The Quartermaster-General has charge of the public *magazines*, store-houses, arsenals, munitions of war, military stores and other military property of the State.

The law forbids the organization of more than twelve volunteer companies of *infantry*, prior to January 1st, 1874, but provides that the number of companies may be increased at the rate of four companies in each year thereafter, until the number of twenty-four companies shall be reached; beyond which, in time of peace, there shall be no increase.

The law provides that each regiment shall consist of a Colonel, a Lieutenant-Colonel, a Major, a Surgeon, an Assistant-Surgeon, a Chaplain, an Adjutant, a Quartermaster-Sergeant, and not less than eight nor more than ten companies ; each of which companies of infantry shall consist of a Captain, a First-Lieutenant, a Second-Lieutenant, five Sergeants, eight Corporals, and not less than thirty-two nor more than seventy privates.

Questions — Who are subject to military duty ? Who are exempt ? How are the militia enrolled ? To what officer do the County Clerks send the number of persons in their respective counties, liable to military duty ? When may the enrolled militia be called into service ? When are the enrolled militia subject to active military duty ? Of whom are the active militia composed ? In case the services of the military are required, what body is first called ? Mention the principal State military officers ? What are the duties of the Adjutant-General ? Of the Inspector-General ? Of the Quartermaster-General ? How many volunteer companies of infantry may be organized ? What officers are required for a regiment ? How many companies in a regiment ? What officers are required for each company ? How many privates ?

CHAPTER XXXV.

OF THE JUDICIAL DEPARTMENT — JUSTICES' COURTS — JURIS-
DICTION — COMMENCEMENT OF SUITS — INCIDENTS OF A
TRIAL.

As people often fail to agree with regard to their *relative* rights and duties, and as they sometimes violate their agreements with each other, and even violate and disobey those rules and regulations *prescribed* for their conduct, it is necessary that *tribunals* should be provided to *administer* justice, to determine and declare the rights of parties, to investigate and decide whether the laws are observed or violated, and to declare and pronounce judgment according to law and the just deserts of the citizen. These determinations are called judicial.

By the Constitution of this State, the Judicial power is vested in one Supreme Court, in Circuit Courts, in Probate Courts, and in Justices of the Peace. *Municipal* courts with civil and criminal jurisdiction may be established by the Legislature in cities.

Justices' Courts — Justices of the Peace are elected for four years. All civil actions, that is, where money is claimed, where the debt or damages claimed do not exceed one hundred dollars, must be brought before Justices of the Peace; and where the amount claimed, in actions upon contract, exceeds one hundred, but does not exceed three hundred dollars, the action may be brought in the Circuit Court or in a Justice's Court ; but a Justice of the Peace has no authority to try actions for a disturbance of a right of way, or for *libel*, or *slander*, or for malicious prosecutions, nor where the title to land is in question, except in certain cases provided for by law.

Actions may be brought before any Justice of the Peace of the city or township,

First — Where the *plaintiffs*, or any of them, reside ; or,

Second—Where the *defendants*, or any of them, reside; or,

Third — Before some justice of another township or city, in the same county, next adjoining the residence of the plaintiff or defendant, or one of the plaintiffs or defendants; or,

Fourth — Before some justice of a city in the same county, formed from a township or townships next adjoining the residence of the plaintiff or defendant, or one of the plaintiffs or defendants.

Persons having matters in difference between them, may go voluntarily before a justice and submit their cause ; but this is seldom done. Suits are usually commenced by *process*, namely, a summons, a warrant, an attachment, or writ of replevin.

A justice's summons is a writing signed by the Justice and addressed to any Constable of the county in which the Justice resides, commanding him to summon the defendant to appear before the Justice at his office, at a certain time named, to answer unto the plaintiff. The officer is required to execute the summons, if the defendant be found, by reading it to him, and (if he require it) delivering him a copy ; but if the defendant be not found, the officer is required to leave a copy of the summons at the defendant's last place of abode, in the presence of some one of the family of suitable age and *discretion*, who shall be informed of its contents.

An attachment, in addition to the summons, contains an order requiring the officer to seize the defendant's property. This, however, is not authorized, unless the plaintiff makes oath, in writing, that the defendant is doing or has done some act mentioned in the law, to *defraud* his creditors, or that he has *absconded* to the injury of his creditors, or does not reside in the State, and has not resided therein for one month immediately preceding the time of applying for the attachment ; or that he *fraudulently contracted* the debt, or *incurred* the *obligation* concerning which suit was brought.

Where a person shows by *affidavit* that he has a claim against another for money collected as a public officer, or for damages arising from the misconduct or neglect of the defendant in any *professional* employment or public office, or that there was fraud or *breach of trust ;* or where the defendant has committed a *trespass* or other wrong, or has *incurred* a *penalty* or *forfeiture* for a violation of some law of this State, such person is entitled to a warrant from the Justice, which authorizes and requires him to arrest the defendant, and to

6

bring him forthwith before the Justice, to answer unto the plaintiff.

In case a person has in his possession property which he has no right to keep, the person who has a right to it, if the property does not exceed in value one hundred dollars, may apply to a Justice for a writ to authorize the Constable to take and deliver such property to the plaintiff. The writ is called a writ of replevin, and after it is executed, the parties have a trial before the Justice, to determine who has the right to the possession of the property. If the plaintiff fails, he must return the property to the defendant, or pay him the value of it.

In whatever way a suit is commenced, a trial must be had, to determine the rights of the parties.

Either party may manage his own case before the Justice, or may have an attorney for that purpose. Before proceeding to the trial, the parties put in their pleadings ; that is, make a statement of their claims. These statements are usually in writing. Making these statements we call, joining *issue*. When this is accomplished, the Justice proceeds to try the issue. Those persons who know about the matters in difference between the parties, are called as witnesses. Before they are permitted to testify, they are required to take a solemn *oath* or affirmation to testify truthfully. The oath is administered, substantially as follows :

The witness is required to raise his right hand, and the Justice then says : " You do solemnly swear that the testimony you shall give upon the trial of the issue now here joined, wherein John Doe is plaintiff and Richard Roe is defendant, shall be the truth, the whole truth, and nothing but the truth. So help you God."

Some people think it wrong to take an oath. In such case, when they are required to give testimony, they *affirm*.

The *affirmation* is administered by the Justice, as follows:
" You do solemnly and sincerely affirm that the testimony you
shall give upon the trial of the issue now here joined, wherein
John Doe is plaintiff and Richard Roe is defendant, shall be
the truth, the whole truth, and nothing but the truth ; this
you will do, under the pains and *penalties* of *perjury*."

After the witnesses have made their statements, and
answered all proper questions put to them, and the parties or
their attorneys have argued the case to the Justice, he decides
it, and records in a book kept for that purpose, called his
docket, his judgment.

Questions — For what purposes are judicial tribunals provided?
In what courts is the Judicial power of the State vested? What civil
actions may be brought before a Justice of the Peace, and what not?
Where may actions be brought before Justices of the Peace? How
are suits commenced? What is a summons? How is the summons
to be executed? What does a writ of attachment contain? What
must a plaintiff show in order to entitle him to a warrant against the
defendant? What does the warrant require? What is the office of a
writ of replevin? When this writ is executed, what is to be done in
the suit? Who may conduct the trial? How do the parties join
issue? What proceedings follow the joining of issue? Give the form
of oath administered to witnesses. Of the affirmation. After the
witnesses have been examined, what does the Justice do?

CHAPTER XXXVI.

OF JURY TRIALS — HOW JUDGMENTS ARE EXECUTED OR SATIS-
FIED —

Whenever a suit is commenced before a Justice of the
Peace, either party desiring it may have it tried by a jury.

A jury in a Justice's Court consists of six men, who are required to sit together before the Justice and hear the proofs and *allegations* of the parties. They take an oath to discharge their duties faithfully. The Justice decides what testimony is proper to be submitted to the Jury. After the parties have introduced all their evidence, and have said, either in person or by attorney, what they desire to say to the Jury, by way of argument, the Jury, under the charge of a Constable, retire to another room and there talk the matter over and agree upon a decision; and when they have thus agreed, they return into Court and inform the Justice what conclusion they have arrived at. This decision is called a verdict, and means a true saying. If the Jury fail to agree, the Justice calls another jury who proceed to try the case, unless the parties consent that the Justice may try it.

When the Jurors have agreed upon their verdict, the Justice makes a record of their decision in his journal, and renders his judgment thereon.

In procuring a jury, the Constable writes down the names of eighteen good men of the county, and each party strikes off or rejects six of the persons named on the list, and those whose names remain, constitute the Jury, who are summoned to appear before the Justice.

The party who fails in the case, is required to pay to the other party his *costs*.

After a judgment has been rendered in any case, it is necessary that it should be enforced. This is done by the Constable, who acts by authority of a written order issued by the Justice, called an execution. Suppose a judgment is rendered in favor of a party for a sum of money : the Justice issues his execution, in which he commands the Constable to *levy* upon the property of the party against whom the judgment was rendered, and to sell enough to pay the debt and costs, and to bring the money to the Justice to be paid to the party entitled thereto.

If either party to a judgment rendered in a Justice's Court, feels that justice has not been done him, he may take an appeal to the Circuit Court. In such case the cause is tried in the Circuit Court as if it had been commenced there. A case may also be removed from a Justice's Court by *certiorari* to the Circuit Court. This is done when a party thinks the proceedings, or some of them, before the Justice were not according to law. In such case a copy of the proceedings, together with a brief memorandum of the testimony, and the decisions of the Justice as to the *admissibility* of any proposed testimony, are sent to the Circuit Court. After inspecting the papers, if the Court thinks the Justice committed no error, his judgment is *affirmed*, but if the judgment was wrong, it is reversed.

Questions — Of how many persons is a jury composed, in a Justice's Court? What are the duties of juries? What is their decision called? If the jury fail to agree, what course is pursued? What is the duty of the Justice when the verdict is rendered? How are jurors procured? How are the judgments of the Justice enforced? Is the judgment of the Justice final? To what courts may causes be removed? In what way? What course is pursued in the Circuit Court, where a cause has been appealed? In case of removal by *certiorari?*

CHAPTER XXXVII.

OF PROCEEDINGS BEFORE JUSTICES OF THE PEACE, IN CRIMINAL CASES.

Justices of the Peace have power to hear and determine certain criminal cases. Among them may be mentioned, *larceny*, where the goods stolen are not worth more than twenty-five dollars; simple *assault* and *battery;* destroying, removing or injuring any *mile-stone* or *mile-board*, or defacing any *inscription* or *device* upon, or doing injury to any *guide-post* or *guide-board; maliciously* killing, *maiming* or *disfiguring* any horses, cattle or other beast of any other person, or injuring or destroying other *personal property*, where the injury done does not exceed twenty-five dollars; destroying or breaking down *monuments* erected for the purpose of designating boundary lines; for *willfully defacing* any building or sign-board; willful trespasses, and all other offenses punishable by fine not exceeding one hundred dollars, or punishable by imprisonment in the county jail not exceeding three months, or punishable by both said fine and imprisonment.

Upon complaint made to any Justice that any of the offenses that may be tried before him have been committed within the county, he is required to examine the person making the complaint under oath, and to reduce the complaint to writing, and have the *complainant* sign it. If it appear that an offense has been committed, he is required to issue his *warrant* for the arrest of the person accused. On being brought before the Justice, the charge is read to him, and if he admits his guilt, the Justice at once renders judgment against him, which judgment fixes the *penalty* the prisoner is to pay or the imprisonment he must suffer. If he does not admit his guilt, the Justice proceeds to try him, unless he demands a trial by jury, in which case a jury of six men are summoned, as in civil cases, before whom the cause is tried.

The Jury determine and decide whether the accused is guilty or not. If they find him guilty, they so declare, and the Justice proceeds to pronounce sentence — that is, to declare what punishment the person convicted shall suffer.

In some cases the law fixes the precise penalty to be

inflicted; but in most cases certain limits are fixed, within which the Justice may exercise his discretion. When the law provides that the punishment shall be by imprisonment, not exceeding ninety days, the Justice may fix the punishment at any length of time not exceeding ninety days.

Justices of the Peace have no authority to try criminal cases where the offense is punishable by a fine exceeding one hundred dollars, or is punishable by imprisonment for more than ninety days. Nevertheless, a Justice has power to cause persons accused of offenses that he cannot try, to be arrested and brought before him; and if, upon examining into the case, he has good cause to suspect that such an offense has been committed, and that the person accused thereof is guilty, he may require him to enter into bonds for his appearance at the next term of the Circuit Court (or if in the city of Detroit, at the next term of the Recorder's Court), and in case he fail or refuse to give such bonds, the Justice is required to make out a written order, called a warrant of commitment, which authorizes the Sheriff of the county to receive and keep the accused in the county jail to await his trial.

Questions—Mention some of the offenses for which a Justice of the Peace may try a person accused. What is the limit of a Justice's jurisdiction with reference to the extent of punishment? When complaint is made to a Justice that an offense has been committed, for which he may try the accused, what is he required to do? May the accused be tried by Jury? If the Jury find the prisoner guilty, what is the Justice required to do? Does the law generally fix the penalty, so as to leave no discretion on the part of the Justice? What discretion is generally given to Justices, in regard to punishment? In relation to those criminal cases which a Justice cannot try, what is his duty?

CHAPTER XXXVIII.

PROBATE COURTS — THEIR GENERAL DUTIES AND POWERS — CIRCUIT COURTS AND SUPREME COURT — THEIR DUTIES AND POWERS.

The duties of Probate Courts pertain, chiefly, to the settlement of the *estates* of *deceased* persons, though some other powers are conferred on this Court by law.

Persons often have reduced to writing what disposition they wish made of their property, and what they desire to be done after their deatn. This writing the person signs his name to, and at his request, two other persons sign their names to the instrument as witnesses. This instrument is called a will. A will, therefore, is " the legal declaration of a man's intentions of what he wills to be performed after his death." A will is sometimes called a testament.

When a will is filed in the office of the Probate Judge, and he is informed of the death of the person who made it, he appoints a time for *proving* it, and if, at the time appointed, it appears to the Court that the testator was of sound mind, and that the will was executed according to law, he so decides, and thereupon makes out and delivers to the person designated in the will for that purpose, or to some other suitable person, letters *testamentary*, or letters of *administration*. The person receiving such letters proceeds to take charge of the estate of the *deceased*, and after paying off debts, if he have any, and expenses of administration, disposes of the residue as provided for in the will.

If a person die without having made a legal will, it is the

duty of the Probate Court, when applied to for that purpose, to appoint some suitable person to take charge of and settle up the business and estate of the deceased. The person so appointed is called an Administrator. Probate Courts have power to appoint guardians for minors, to adjudicate and determine who are the heirs of deceased persons, in certain cases ; to entertain proceedings for the condemnation of lands for railroads, and to do and perform many other acts prescribed by law.

Circuit Courts. — The State is divided into twenty judicial circuits, and a Circuit Judge is elected in each circuit, who holds his term of office for six years.

Circuit Courts are held in each organized county at least twice in each year, and four times in each year in those counties having ten thousand inhabitants.

All civil actions and remedies of whatever name or description, and all prosecutions for *crimes, misdemeanors, offenses* and *penalties*, except in cases where by law some other court or *tribunal* has *jurisdiction*, are to be commenced, heard and determined in the Circuit Courts.

Cases tried in Justices' Courts and proceedings had in Probate Courts may be appealed to the Circuit Courts. The Circuit Court has general *supervisory jurisdiction* over all inferior tribunals.

Causes tried in the Circuit Court may, if either party desires it, be tried by a jury of twelve men. All criminal causes in the Circuit Court must be tried by a jury.

The Circuit Courts have *equity* or *chancery* powers, and when acting as a court in what we call *equity* cases, we refer to it as the Circuit Court in Chancery. The courts of law are limited in their proceedings to certain *actions*, and according to certain rules. In most cases these actions and rules will enable the courts to do justice by the parties. But as in some cases justice cannot be done to the parties in any of the forms of action known to the courts of law, the case must be submitted to a court not bound by such strict rules.

The courts of law render a general judgment, that a party recover a certain sum of money, or the possession of certain property. The law then directs how that judgment shall be enforced.

The decision or determination of a Court of Chancery is called a decree. This decree, unlike a simple judgment, often contains qualifications, conditions and arrangements to be carried out in the future — such conditions and arrangements as, under the circumstances of the particular case, are just and *equitable*.

Supreme Court. — This Court consists of four Justices, who hold their offices for eight years. The people elect one of these Justices every two years, at the Spring election.

The one whose term of office first expires, acts as Chief Justice.

The following will show the names of the present (1874) Justices of the Supreme Court, and the times at which their terms of office will expire :

BENJAMIN F. GRAVES, December 31, 1875.
THOMAS M. COOLEY,   "   " 1877.
JAMES V. CAMPBELL,   "   " 1879.
ISAAC P. CHRISTIANCY,   "   " 1881.

The Supreme Court has a general superintending control over all the other courts of the State, to prevent and correct errors and abuses therein. Where, for instance, a Circuit Court has determined a matter pending before it, and a party in interest conceives that in the investigation or determination, the Court has erred in applying the rules of law, the case may be removed to the Supreme Court for review and correction.

In cases tried before the Circuit Court in Chancery, an appeal may be taken to the Supreme Court. In case persons are wrongfully *restrained* of their liberty, the Supreme Court has power to discharge them. If inferior courts refuse to discharge duties required of them by law, the Supreme Court has power to compel them to proceed; or, it may prevent them from proceeding in a matter without legal authority.

Where it is claimed that inferior courts or tribunals have proceeded in a matter different from the course *prescribed* by law, the Supreme Court may compel such court or tribunal to certify and send up its proceedings, and thereupon that Court may correct the error, if any has been committed.

The Supreme Court holds four terms each year, at the Capital.

Questions — To what do the duties of the Probate Court chiefly pertain? What is a will? What is the duty of the Probate Judge in relation to the proving of wills? If a person die without a will, what is the duty of the Probate Court in relation to the property of the deceased? What are some of the other powers of Probate Courts? Into how many judicial circuits is the State divided? What is the term for which Circuit Judges are elected? How often are the Circuit Courts held in each organized county? What is the *jurisdiction* of Circuit Courts? What is the number of jurors required to try a cause in the Circuit Court? May criminal causes in the Circuit Court, be tried without a jury?

When is the Circuit Court said to be sitting as a Court of Chancery? What is the necessity or occasion for Courts of Chancery? What do we call the decision of a Court of Chancery? Wherein does it differ from a judgment in a Court of Law? Of how many justices is the Supreme Court composed? Which Justice acts as Chief Justice? Name the Justices and times when their terms of office will expire. What is the general jurisdiction of the Supreme Court? Where are the sessions of the Supreme Court held? How many terms of the Supreme Court are held each year?

CHAPTER XXXIX.

PUBLIC INSTRUCTION — DISTRICT SCHOOLS — SCHOOL OFFICERS,
THEIR POWERS — PENALTY FOR FAILURE TO SEND CHIL-
DREN TO SCHOOL.

The various townships of the State are divided into school districts, by School Inspectors. The district officers are a Moderator, a Director, and an Assessor.

The voters of the district are required to meet together on the first Monday of September in each year, to elect a district officer, and to vote upon such other matters as may be legally brought before them. Other meetings may be called for certain purposes.

The school officers hold their terms of office for three years ; the Moderator being elected one year, the Director the next year, and the Assessor the next, and so on.

The persons qualified to vote at a school meeting are, all electors at a township meeting, and every person, three months a resident in the district, and twenty-one years of age, liable to pay a district tax, whether male or female. The voters at a regular school meeting may *designate* a *site* for a school-house, or may change such site by a similar vote. The voters also have power to direct the purchasing or leasing of such site ; also the building, hiring, or purchasing of a school-house ; but unless the number of children in the district, between the ages of five and twenty years, shall exceed fifty, no more than one thousand dollars shall be raised for such purpose in any one year.

The Moderator, Director, and Assessor constitute the District Board. It is their duty to hire teachers ; to buy school books for poor children ; to determine what books shall be used in the schools ; to report to the Supervisor the amount of money to be raised by tax for the support of the school, and may establish all needful regulations for its management.

By a special act of 1873, Berrien county has a County Board to prescribe, and contract for, uniform text-books throughout the county.

School districts containing more than one hundred children between the ages of five and twenty years, may elect a District Board to consist of six trustees. Such trustees have power to *classify* and *grade* the scholars in their district, and cause them to be taught in such schools or *departments* as they may *deem expedient;* to establish a High School, when ordered by a vote of the district, and to perform such other duties as are usually performed by the District Board already mentioned.

It is made, by law, the duty of parents and others having the charge of any child or children, between the ages of eight and fourteen years, to send such child or children, if able to attend, to a public school for a period of at least twelve weeks in each year ; and a failure to do so subjects them to a fine of not less than five nor more than ten dollars for the first offense, nor less than ten nor more than twenty dollars for the second, and every subsequent offense.

Questions — Into what districts do School Inspectors divide townships? At what time is the annual district meeting held? For what purpose is it held? Name the school officers and their terms of office. What are the qualifications of voters at a school meeting? Mention some of the powers of voters at a school meeting. Who constitute the District Board? Mention some of their duties. What body prescribes text-books for the schools of Berrien county? What is said of other districts? What does the law require of parents and others in relation to sending children under their charge to school? What is the *penalty* for a failure to comply with the provisions of this law?

CHAPTER XL.

THE STATE NORMAL SCHOOL — STATE UNIVERSITY — AGRICUL-
TURAL COLLEGE — STATE PUBLIC SCHOOL.

State Normal School.—This was established and designed
to prepare persons for teaching.

After a person has attended the Normal School for
twenty-two weeks, such person, if *qualified*, is entitled to a
certificate to that effect from the Principal, to be approved
by the Superintendent of Public Instruction.

By an Act of the Legislature of 1871, it is provided that
the State Board of Education may grant *diplomas* to such
students as shall have completed the full course of instruction
in the Normal School, and shall have been recommended by
the Board of Instruction.

The person receiving such diploma is entitled to a certificate from the Board of Instruction, which shall serve as a
legal certificate of qualification to teach in the primary schools
of any township in this State.

The Normal School is supported, in part, from the interest
arising from moneys realized from the sale of twenty-five
sections of land *appropriated* for its support in 1849.

University of Michigan.—In 1826, Congress appropriated
two entire townships of land for the establishment of a University in Michigan. Soon after the State was organized, the
University was established.

The law provides that the University shall consist of at
least three departments :

1. A department of literature, science and the arts ;
2. A department of law ;

3. A department of medicine ;

4. Such other departments may be added as the Regent shall deem necessary, and the state of the University fund shall allow.

The number of professors employed in the University is from thirty-five to forty. The students in attendance each year, range from twelve hundred to fourteen hundred.

The State Agricultural College. — This institution is also under the control of the State, and is, in part, supported by funds realized from the sale of lands granted for that purpose. It was established to afford thorough instruction in *agriculture* and the *natural sciences* connected therewith.

Persons to be admitted into this school, must be over fifteen years of age, and pass a satisfactory examination in arithmetic, geography, grammar, reading, spelling, and penmanship.

There is a farm connected with the institution, on which students are required to labor three hours in each day.

Questions — For what purpose was the State Normal School established? What is said of the granting of diplomas? To what is the person receiving this diploma entitled? How is the Normal School supported? What appropriations did Congress make for the establishment of a University in Michigan? Of what departments does the law require the University to consist? How many professors are employed in the University? How many students usually attend, each year? For what purpose was the State Agricultural College established? What is required of applicants for admission? What is required in regard to labor?

CHAPTER XLI.

OF BENEVOLENT INSTITUTIONS.

The State Public School for dependent and neglected children, is located at Coldwater, and is supported by the State. The object in establishing this institution was to furnish temporary homes for dependent and neglected children; especially those who have been abandoned by their parents or are orphans, or whose parents have been convicted of crime. The children in this school are educated in the branches usually taught in common schools.

It is made the duty of the Board of Control to use all diligence to provide suitable places, in good families, for the children who are inmates of the school.

The Michigan Institution for Educating Deaf and Dumb, and Blind persons is located at Flint, and is under the control of a Board of Trustees.

Tuition and board are free to all *candidates* from this State; and where such persons, on account of poverty, are unable to furnish themselves with suitable clothing and other necessary expenses for attending the school, the Board of Trustees are authorized to render them assistance not exceeding forty dollars per annum, for each person, to be paid out of the State treasury. This institution is supported by the State.

The Michigan Asylum for the Insane, located at Kalamazoo, is also a State institution, under the control of a Board of Trustees, who appoint a medical superintendent and other officers.

County Superintendents of the Poor, or any Supervisor

of any city or town to which a person who is insane is charge-able, may send such person to the Asylum, and the expense of sending and keeping him there is paid by the town or county to which he is chargeable.

When a person who is *indigent*, but not a *pauper*, be-comes insane, the Probate Judge may send him to the Asylum. In such case the county pays the expenses of his support.

If a person who is an inmate of the Asylum, has means to enable him to do so, he is personally liable for his support in the Asylum.

In 1873, the Legislature provided for the establishment of an additional asylum for the insane, and Pontiac has been selected as the place for its location.

In most of the older counties, poor-houses have been erected, where persons unable to support themselves are kept and provided for at the expense of the county. In other counties they are supported at the expense of the townships.

Questions—Where is the State Public School located? For what purpose was this institution established? In what branches are the children in this school required to be educated? What is required of the Board of Control, with respect to the care of the inmates? Where is the Michigan Institution for Educating Deaf and Dumb, and Blind persons located? On what terms are persons admitted who reside in this State? What *pecuniary* aid may be rendered poor persons who attend this institution? Where is the Michigan Asylum for the Insane located? What officers are authorized to send to the Asylum insane persons who are paupers? What officer may send insane persons who are indigent but not paupers? How are the inmates of the Asylum supported? What provision has been made for an additional asylum? What provision has been made for poor persons?

7

CHAPTER XLII.

PENAL AND REFORMATORY INSTITUTIONS.

Penal and reformatory institutions have been found necessary for the punishment and reformation of those who commit crime. They are also necessary to restrain offenders and thereby deprive them of the opportunity or power to violate the law.

A State prison has been established at Jackson where persons convicted of a higher grade of offenses—that is, those crimes that are considered most *atrocious* and wicked—are sent by the Courts for punishment. The prisoners are required to labor and are taught some of the *mechanical* trades.

The prison is under the direction of three Inspectors, appointed by the Governor. The officers of the prison consist of an agent, who is principal keeper of the prison, a clerk, a physician and surgeon, a chaplain, a deputy keeper, and a number of assistant keepers.

The Reform School at Lansing is designed for the reformation of boys, who, between the ages of ten and sixteen years, are convicted of crime.

Persons sent to this institution are sentenced to remain there until they are twenty-one years of age; but the Board of Control have power to discharge them at any time when satisfied of their reformation, or, when their presence in the school is prejudicial to the discipline thereof, may send them back to the Court for punishment in some other institution.

The design of the Reform School is not so much for punishment, as reformation; and the persons sent there are *disci-*

plined, instructed, employed and governed, in such a way as shall tend to make them good citizens.

The Detroit House of Correction was built by the city of Detroit; but by a law of the State, the Board of Supervisors of any county may make an agreement with the Common Council or agent of the city of Detroit, for the confinement of persons convicted of crimes which would otherwise *subject* them to imprisonment in the County Jail, in the House of Correction. In such case the county where the person is convicted pays the city of Detroit for keeping the prisoner.

All females convicted of offenses, except murder, which would, under the general provisions of law, subject them to imprisonment in the State Prison, are sent to the Detroit House of Correction.

In 1871, the Legislature authorized the establishment by the county of Jackson, of a House of Correction, similar to the one established in Detroit.

In each of the organized counties in this State, the law provides for the *erection* of jails for the *detention* of persons accused of crime until they can be tried, and for the punishment of such as are convicted of *minor* offenses.

Prisons are also established in cities and villages, for the confinement of those who violate the by-laws and ordinances.

Where is the State Prison located? What class of offenders are confined there? What officers control the prison? Where is the Reform School located? What persons are sent to this school? What authority has the Board of Control in relation to the custody of the inmates? What is the design of the Reform School? What is said of the Detroit House of Correction? In what institution are female offenders incarcerated? What is said of jails? Of prisons, in cities and villages?

CHAPTER XLIII.

ASSESSMENT AND COLLECTION OF TAXES.

A tax is a contribution which individuals are required to make for the use or service of the State.

Since it is the duty of the Government to protect and defend the people in the enjoyment of their property, it is but just that those who have the most property should pay the largest tax.

As a basis for taxation, the value of all the *real* and *personal property* in the State, except such as the law *exempts*, is estimated, and a certain percentage of its value is required to be paid as a tax, by the owner, or persons in the possession of such property.

The following property is exempt from taxation : Two hundred and fifty dollars' worth of household furniture ; fifty dollars' worth of spinning and weaving looms and *apparatus ;* all arms required to be kept by law, and the clothing of every person or family ; one hundred and fifty dollars' worth of library books, school books, and all family pictures ; to every *householder*, fifteen sheep, with their fleeces, and the yarn and cloth manufactured therefrom ; two cows, five swine, and food and *fuel* sufficient for the family for six months; a hundred dollars' worth of musical instruments ; property of the United States and of this State ; all public or corporate property of counties, cities, villages, townships, and school districts ; the personal property of all library, benevolent, charitable, and scientific associations, incorporated within this State, and lands belonging to or leased by such institutions and occupied by them ; churches, and church property, and places of burial ; and the personal and real estate of persons who, by reason of *infirmity*, age or poverty, may, in the opinion of the Supervisor, be unable to contribute towards the public charges.

When a tenant, paying rent for real estate, shall be taxed therefor, he may retain, out of his rent, the taxes paid by him for the same, unless there be an agreement to the contrary.

It is the duty of the Supervisor, who acts as Assessor, on or before the first Monday in May, of each year, to call upon each person in his township, liable to be taxed, and leave with him a blank form on which to make out statements of the taxable property in his possession ; after which the Supervisor is required to take the list and set down the value of the property embraced in the statement, and deduct from the moneys at interest and other credits of such person, the amount of money upon which he or she pays interest, together with his or her other indebtedness.

On the third Monday of May, and the two following days, persons who are not satisfied with the assessment as made by the Supervisor, may appear before him and show cause why the valuation should be changed. If satisfied he has committed an error, it is his duty to make the proper correction.

After all needed corrections are made, the Supervisor makes out an assessment roll, containing the names of the resident persons liable to be taxed ; a full description of the real estate of such persons ; the number of acres in each tract or parcel, and the *aggregate* valuation of the personal estate of such person, liable to be taxed, as appears from the statements in the possession of the Supervisor.

Lands not occupied and not claimed to be owned by any one living in the township are set down and assessed as *nonresident* lands.

The Township Clerk who keeps the records of the township meetings, and of the meetings of the Township Board, and who keeps files of all orders and votes for raising moneys in his township, furnishes the Supervisor with a statement of the amount of money proposed to be raised, and for what purposes. This statement the Supervisor gives to the County Clerk, who is clerk of the Board of Supervisors.

At their meeting in October, the Board of Supervisors ascertain whether the valuations in the different towns and cities are relatively equal. If they are not they correct them.

The Auditor-General of the State *apportions* the State tax *equitably* among the several counties, and notifies the County Clerks of the amounts required from their respective counties. The Boards of Supervisors apportion the taxes required for county purposes among the townships. In this way the County Clerk is enabled to determine just how much money is to be raised in each township for taxes, and informs the Supervisor, who then assesses the taxes against the individual valuations of property on his assessment roll, specifying what such taxes are required for. This list the Supervisor delivers to the Township Treasurer, who collects the tax.

If persons against whom a tax is assessed, refuse or neglect to pay the same, provision is made by law to sell so much of their property as may be necessary for that purpose; and if the tax assessed against non-resident lands shall not be paid, such lands may be sold to pay the same.

Under our statutes, State, county and township taxes upon real estate, become a lien upon the land from the first Monday in December of the year in which they are assessed, and not before; and as between seller and purchaser under a warranty deed, the obligation is upon the purchaser to pay the taxes for the current year where the conveyance is prior to that date, and upon the vendor, where it is subsequent.

Questions—What is a tax? What is the basis for taxing property? What property is exempt from taxation? What remedy has a tenant who is taxed for the property he rents? In what way does the Assessor ascertain what property is to be assessed for taxation? What provision is made for correcting the Assessor's estimates of value? What does the assessment roll contain? How are unoccupied lands, not claimed by any one in the township, assessed? How does the Clerk of the Board of Supervisors ascertain what is proposed to be raised as a tax for township purposes? How are the valuations of property in the different townships equalized? What officer apportions the State tax among the counties? What body apportions the county tax among the townships? In what way is the Supervisor informed of the amount of tax to be raised in his township? What apportionment does the Supervisor make? What officer collects the tax? In case the tax is not paid, how may the tax be collected? When do the taxes assessed become a lien upon the land? What is said of the obligations of the sellers and purchasers of land, as to the payment of taxes?

CHAPTER XLIV.

TITLE TO REAL PROPERTY BY DESCENT.

When any person shall die *seized* of any lands, *tenements*, or *hereditaments*, or of any right thereto, or entitled to any interest therein, in fee simple, or for the life of another, not having lawfully *devised* the same, they shall descend, subject to his debts, in manner following:

First — In equal shares to his children, and to the *issue* of any deceased child by right of representation; and if there be no child of the *intestate* living at his death, his estate shall descend to all his other *lineal* descendants; and if all the said descendants are in the same degree of *kindred* to the intestate, they shall share the estate equally; otherwise they shall take according to the right of representation.

When we say "property descends in equal shares to a deceased person's children, and to the issue of any deceased child by right of representation," we mean that the issue of the deceased child take the share that would have belonged to such child had he been living. Thus a person dies leaving three children, and three grandchildren, the issue of a deceased child. Each of the three living children would take one fourth of the estate, and each of the grandchildren one twelfth. The three grandchildren thus represent or stand in the place of the deceased child, and hence we say, "they take by right of representation."

Inheritance, or succession, by "right of representation," takes place when the descendants of any deceased heir take the same share or right in the estate of another person that their parent would have taken if living. *Posthumous* children are considered as living at the death of their parents.

Second — If he shall leave no issue, his estate shall descend to his widow during her natural lifetime, and, after her decease, to his father; and if he shall leave no issue or widow, his estate shall descend to his father;

Third — If he shall leave no issue, nor widow, nor father, his estate shall descend in equal shares to his brothers and sisters, and to the children of any deceased brother or sister, by right of representation: *Provided*, That if he shall leave a mother also, she shall take an equal share with his brothers and sisters ;

Fourth — If the intestate shall leave no issue, nor widow, nor father, and no brother nor sister living at his death, his estate shall descend to his mother, to the exclusion of the issue, if any, of deceased brothers or sisters ;

Fifth — If the intestate shall leave no issue nor widow,

and no father, mother, brother, nor sister, his estate shall descend to his next of kin in equal degree, excepting that when there are two or more collateral kindred in equal degree, but claiming through different *ancestors*, those who claim through the nearest ancestor shall be preferred to those claiming through an ancestor more remote: *Provided however*,

Sixth—If any person shall die leaving several children, or leaving one child, and the issue of one or more other children, and any such surviving child shall die under age, and not having been married, all the estate that came to the deceased child by inheritance from such deceased parent shall descend in equal shares to the other children of the same parent, and to the issue of any such other children who shall have died, by right of representation ;

Seventh—If, at the death of such child who shall die under age, and not having been married, all the other children of his said parent shall also be dead, and any of them shall have left issue, the estate that came to said child by inheritance from his said parent shall descend to all the issue of other children of the same parent ; and if all the said issue are in the same degree of kindred to said child, they shall share the said estate equally, otherwise they shall take according to the right of representation ;

Eighth—If the intestate shall leave a widow and no kindred, his estate shall descend to such widow ;

Ninth—If the intestate shall leave no widow nor kindred, his estate shall *escheat* to the people of this State, for the use of the primary school fund.

Any estate, real or personal, that may have been given by the intestate in his lifetime, as an advancement to any child or other lineal descendant, shall be considered as a part of the estate of the intestate, so far as it regards the division and distribution thereof among his issue, and shall be taken by such child or other descendants toward his share of the estate of the intestate.

All gifts and grants shall be deemed to have been made in advancement, if they are expressed in the gift or grant to be so made, or if charged in writing by the intestate as an advancement, or acknowledged in writing as such by the child or other descendant.

If any child, or other lineal descendant, so advanced, shall die before the intestate, leaving issue, the advancement shall be taken into consideration, in the division and distribution of the estate, and the amount thereof shall be allowed accordingly, by the representatives of the heir so advanced, in like manner as if the advancement had been made directly to them.

Questions — Define the word seized, as use   in this chapter. Tenements.   Hereditaments.   Devise.   Issue.   Intestate.   Lineal. Kindred.   Ancestor.   When a person dies without a will, to whom does his property descend, first?   When we say property descends in equal shares to a deceased person's children, and to the issue of any deceased child by right of representation, what do we mean?   When does inheritance, or succession, by "right of representation," take place?

If a man die leaving no issue, how does his estate descend?   If he leave no issue or widow?   If he leave no issue, nor widow nor father? If he leave no issue, nor widow nor father, and no brother nor sister living at his death?   If he leave no issue nor widow, and no father, mother, brother nor sister?   If he leave several children or one child, and the issue of one or more other children, and any such surviving child shall die under age and not having been married, what becomes of the share inherited by the deceased child from his parent?   If, in the case just mentioned, all the other children of said parent shall also be dead and any of them shall have left issue, to whom does the estate that came to said child by such inheritance go?   When does the estate descend to the widow?   When does the property escheat to the people of the State?   What is said of gifts by way of advancement?   When shall gifts or grants be deemed to have been made in advancement? In case of the death of the person to whom an advancement is made before the death of the person making it, what is done with such advancement?

CHAPTER XLV.

OF WEIGHTS AND MEASURES.

The law of this State provides how many pounds of certain grain, dried fruit, coal, vegetables and products, shall constitute a bushel: Wheat, 60 ; rye, 56 ; shelled corn, 56 ; corn on the cob, 70 ; corn meal, 50 ; oats, 32 ; buckwheat, 48 ; beans, 60; clover seed, 60 ; timothy seed, 45; flax seed, 56 ; hemp seed, 44; millet, 50 ; Hungarian grass seed, 50 ; blue grass seed, 14 ; barley, 48 ; dried apples, 22 ; dried peaches, 28 ; potatoes, 60 ; sweet potatoes, 56 ; onions, 54; turnips, 58 ; peas, 60 ; cranberries, 40 ; dried plums, 28; castor beans, 46 ; Michigan salt, 56 ; mineral coal, 80 ; orchard grass seed, 14 ; Osage orange seed, 33 ; stone lime, 70 ; red-top seed, 14.

A box or basket of peaches must contain seven hundred and sixteen and three-fourths cubic inches, or one-third of a bushel.

. A barrel of fruit, roots or vegetables, is that quantity contained in a barrel made from staves twenty-seven inches in length, and each head sixteen and one-half inches in diameter.

All wheat flour, rye flour, and buckwheat meal, manufactured in this State for sale or exportation, shall be packed in good and strong casks, made of seasoned oak or other sufficient timber, and hooped with at least ten good and substantial hoops, three of which shall be on each chime, and properly nailed.

The casks shall be of two sizes, one of which shall contain one hundred and ninety-six pounds of flour or meal, with staves twenty-seven inches in length, and each head sixteen and one-half inches in diameter ; the other size shall contain ninety-eight pounds, with staves twenty-two inches long, and each head fourteen inches in diameter.

The casks shall be made as nearly straight as may be, and their *tare* shall be accurately marked on one head with a marking iron, and they shall also be branded with the weight of the flour or meal contained therein, and with the initials of the Christian and the whole of the surname of the manufacturers thereof, except when such flour or meal shall be manufactured by a company, when the cask may be branded with the name of such company.

Every such cask of wheat flour shall also be branded as follows, namely : If of a superior quality, " Superfine," if of a second quality, " Fine," if of a third quality, " Fine middlings," if of a fourth quality, " Middlings."

Each cask of rye flour of the first quality shall be branded with the words " Superfine rye flour," and each cask of the second quality, with the words " Fine rye flour," and each cask of buckwheat meal shall be branded with the words " B. meal."

Questions — Give the weight per bushel of the different grains, fruits and products mentioned in this lesson.   What is the size required for a box or basket of peaches ?   State the size required for barrels of fruit, roots or vegetables.   In what way must wheat flour, rye flour and buckwheat meal be packed ?   What is said of the sizes and capacity of casks ?   How are the casks to be made and branded ?   What brands are to be placed on casks of wheat flour ?   Of rye flour ?   Of buckwheat meal ?

CHAPTER XLVI.

THE PUBLIC HEALTH.

The Supervisor and Justices of the Peace constitute a Board of Health for the township in which they reside.

The Board has power to appoint a physician as a Health Officer, and may make such regulations concerning *nuisances*, sources of filth, and causes of sickness, within their townships, and on board of any vessels in their ports or harbors, as they shall judge necessary for the public health and safety; and if any person shall violate any such regulations, he shall forfeit a sum not exceeding one hundred dollars. The Board of Health are required to give notice of their regulations by publishing the same in some newspaper of the township, if there be one published therein, and if not, by posting them up in five public places in the township.

It is the duty of the Board to make provision to prevent the spread of the small-pox, or other dangerous diseases; and for this purpose may cause any sick or *infected* person to be removed to a separate house, if it can be done without injury to his health ; and if necessary, they may cause the persons in the neighborhood to be removed. They may take possession of convenient houses and lodgings for the sick, and may employ nurses, and attendants, and procure other necessaries for them.

The inhabitants may, if they desire, establish *hospitals* in any township, for the reception of persons having the small-pox or other diseases which may be dangerous to the public health.

In cities, the Mayor and Aldermen, and in incorporated villages, the President and Trustees, constitute the Board of Health.

Questions — What officers constitute the Board of Health in townships? What are the powers of the Board in regard to establishing regulations to prevent the spread of disease? What is said of hospitals? What officers constitute the Board of Health in cities? In villages?

CHAPTER XLVII.

OF FENCES AND FENCE-VIEWERS — WHEN NO DAMAGES ALLOWED FOR INJURIES BY TRESPASSING ANIMALS.

All fences four and a half feet high, in good repair, consisting of rails, timber, boards or stone walls, or any combination thereof, and all brooks, rivers, ponds, creeks, ditches, and hedges, or other things which shall be considered equivalent thereto, in the judgment of the Fence-Viewers within whose jurisdiction the same may be, shall be deemed legal and sufficient fences.

It is the duty of persons occupying adjoining lands, to maintain partition fences, in equal shares, so long as both parties continue to improve such lands. The Overseers of Highways are, by law, made the Fence-Viewers in their respective townships, and it is their duty, when the parties cannot agree, to determine the condition of partition fences, and to assign to the parties their share of such fences to be by them kept in repair.

The law provides that no person shall be entitled to recover any sum of money, in any action at law, for damages done upon lands by any beast or beasts, unless the partition fences by which such lands are wholly or in part enclosed, and belonging to such person, or by him to be kept in repair, shall be of the same height and description as is required by the provisions of the first paragraph of this chapter.

Questions — What constitutes a lawful fence? What is the duty of persons occupying adjoining lands, with reference to partition fences? Who constitute the Fence-Viewers, and what are their duties? What is said with reference to the recovery of damages for injuries from trespassing animals?

CHAPTER XLVIII.

MONEY AND INTEREST.

The interest of money shall be at the rate of seven dollars upon one hundred dollars for a year, and at the same rate for a greater or less sum, and for a longer or shorter time. But it is lawful for the parties to stipulate in writing any rate of interest not exceeding ten per cent. per annum.

Where parties agree that the rate of interest shall exceed that authorized by law, the legal rate, and no more, can be recovered, in an action at law.

When any *installment* of interest upon any note, bond, mortgage, or other written contract shall become due, and the same shall remain unpaid, interest may be computed and collected on any such installment so due and unpaid, from the time at which it becomes due, at the same rate as specified in any such note, bond, mortgage or other written *contract*, not exceeding ten per cent., and if no rate of interest be specified, then at the rate of seven per cent. per annum.

Parties loaning money, may take interest authorized by the law of this State, without reference to the law of the place where the money may be payable.

Questions — What is the legal rate of interest in Michigan? What rate may parties agree upon? Where the rate of interest agreed upon exceeds that authorized by law, what may be recovered? What is said of interest upon installments? When money loaned in this State is made payable elsewhere, what rate of interest may be taken?

CHAPTER XLIX.

OF THE SUPPORT OF POOR PERSONS.

The father, mother, and children of any poor person who is blind, old, lame, *impotent* or *decrepit*, so as to be unable to maintain himself, shall, at their own charge, relieve and maintain such poor person, in such manner as shall be approved by the Directors of the Poor of the township where such poor person may be, or by the Superintendents of the County Poor.

If the relatives whose duty it is to provide for a poor person, refuse to do so, the Circuit Court may make an order to compel them to furnish such support.

The father shall be first required to maintain such poor person, if of sufficient ability; if there be no father, or if he be not of sufficient ability, then the children of such poor person; if there be no such children, or they be not of sufficient ability, then the mother, if she be able to do so.

If the relative required by law to support a poor person, is unable wholly to maintain such poor person, the Court has power to direct two or more relatives to furnish such support, and may fix the amount to be furnished by each.

When parents abandon their children and refuse to support them, or when a husband so abandons his wife, the Superintendents of the Poor may seize upon the property of such parent or husband, and the same may be sold for the support of such wife and children.

The personal property of paupers, except their wearing apparel, may be sold for their support.

When poor persons, unable to support themselves, have no relatives able to support them, they may be supported at the expense of the county. If the poor person needs *temporary* relief only, it may be furnished by the Supervisor of the township, city, or ward, or by the Superintendents of the Poor; but if the person requires *permanent* relief, he is, in those counties having poor-houses, to be taken to such poor-house, where he is kept and supported under the directions of the Superintendents.

In some of the counties the distinction between township and county poor has not been abolished by the Board of Supervisors. In such cases it is the duty of the township to provide for such of their citizens as are unable to support themselves, unless their relatives are able to furnish such support.

Questions—What relatives are required to support poor persons? May relatives, having the ability so to do, be required to support poor persons? State the order in which relatives are required to support poor persons. In case a relative whose duty it is, by law, to support a poor person, is unable to provide sufficient support, what order may the Circuit Court make? What is said concerning those who abandon their children and wives and refuse to support them? What may be done with the personal property of paupers? In case a person is unable to support himself, and has no relatives able to do so, what provision is made?

CHAPTER L.

OF THE LIEN OF MECHANICS AND OTHERS.

For the purpose of enabling mechanics and others who may furnish labor or materials for constructing or repairing buildings, or for putting up any engine, machinery, or *appurtenances*, for the owner or *lessee* of lands, upon such lands, the law has provided for a *lien* thereon.

Such lien shall not attach, unless the contractor, or some one in his behalf, shall make and file with the Register of Deeds of the county in which the land shall lie, a certificate containing a copy of his contract, if the same is in his possession and in writing, and if not, then a statement of the terms of the contract, as near as he can give it, and a description of the piece or pieces lot or lots of land, on which such building, wharf, or machinery shall be or is to be constructed or put up, and a statement of the amount due and to become due, on said contract, together with all credits the owner may be entitled to, which certificate shall be verified by the affidavit of the contractor, or some one in his behalf. When this is done, and the owner is notified thereof, the lien becomes binding.

The lien, when the certificate has been recorded, continues good for six months, when it ceases, unless proceedings shall, within that time, be taken to enforce the lien.

Sub-contractors may also have a lien for work and materials furnished by them. This is secured by making and filing with the Register of Deeds a similar certificate to that required of the contractor, and containing a further statement of the terms of his contract with the original contractor.

The person desirous of enforcing the lien, prepares and presents to the Circuit Court in Chancery, for the county in which the land may lie, a petition containing a brief statement of the contract or contracts, and of the amount due thereon, with a description of the premises subject to the lien, and all other material facts and circumstances, and praying for a sale or other disposition of the premises to satisfy the same.

This petition should not be filed until the expiration of sixty days from the maturity of the debt. The Court has power to direct the giving of such notice to the owner, of the time of hearing, as may be considered just. This notice should embrace a copy of the order of the Court and of the petition, and should be personally served, if the owner lives in this State. Notice should also be given to other creditors who have similar liens upon the same property. If the owner lives out of the State, the Court directs the notice to be given by publishing the same in some newspaper printed or circulating within the county, for six successive weeks.

At the time fixed for the hearing, the creditors appear before the Court and prove their claims, and the Court determines the amount due to each creditor who has a lien upon the property in question, and may order a sale of such property to satisfy the claims.

By the law of 1871, provision is made for the better security of mechanics and other persons furnishing materials for the erecting, altering, repairing, beautifying, or ornamenting of buildings. By this provision the lien may include the building and land on which it stands, not exceeding a quarter of a section, to the extent of the interest of the owner or lessee thereof. This act may be found in a note following this chapter.

Liens Upon Personal Property.—Mechanics, artisans, and tradesmen may retain and have a lien for labor and mate-

rial furnished by them in constructing or repairing any article
of value.

Any person may have a lien upon horses, cattle, mules,
sheep, or swine for their keeping, and may retain possession
of them until the charges are paid.

In order to enforce these liens, suits may be brought
before a Justice of the Peace, and judgment recovered for
such charges. Thereupon an execution is issued and the property retained, sold to satisfy the lien.

Questions—For what has the law furnished a lien? What are the
conditions upon which the lien attaches? How long does the lien
continue? What is said of sub-contractors? How is the lien enforced?
What is said of giving notice to the owner? What is said of the law
of 1871? What is said of liens upon personal property?

Note.—*Act of* 1871. Section 1. *The People of the State of Michigan enact*, That
every mechanic, workman, or other person, who shall hereafter, in conformity with
the terms of the contract between the owner or lessee of any lot or piece of ground,
or his agent, and the original contractor or any sub-contractor, perform any labor,
or furnish any materials in building, altering, repairing, beautifying, or ornamenting any house or other building, or machinery, or appurtenances to any house or
other building, in this State, shall have a lien for the value of such labor and materials upon such house or building and appurtenances, and upon the lot of land upon
which the same stands, not exceeding one-quarter of a section, including such
building, to the extent of the right, title, and interest of such owner or lessee, at
the time of the making the original contract for such house or the improvements;
but the aggregate of all the liens hereby authorized shall not exceed the price
stipulated in the original contract between such owner or lessee and the original
contractor, for such improvements; in no case shall the owner or lessee be compelled to pay a greater sum for or on account of such house, building, or other
improvement, than the price or sum stipulated in said original contract or agreement.

Sec. 2. The person performing such labor, or furnishing such materials, shall
cause a notice, in writing, to be served on such owner or lessee, or his agent, substantially in the following form: " To ——: You are hereby notified that I am (or have
been) employed by ——, as a laborer (or have furnished materials, or am about to
furnish materials) on or for your house, or building, and that I shall hold the house,
building, and your interest in the ground, liable for my services thereon (or materials furnished)." If there shall be a contract, in writing, between the original
contractor and the sub-contractor, or between the original contractor and the person so performing labor or furnishing materials as aforesaid, a copy of such sub-
contract, if the same can be obtained, shall be served with such notice and attached

thereto, which notice shall be served within twenty days from the completion of such contract, or within twenty days after payment should have been made to the person performing such labor or furnishing such material.

SEC. 3. In all cases where the owner or lessee, or his or their agent, cannot be found in the county in which said improvements shall be made, or shall not reside therein, the person furnishing labor or materials shall file said notice in the office of the register of deeds of said county, and the said register shall enter, in a book kept by him for that purpose, alphabetically, the names of the owners or lessees, and opposite thereto, the names of the persons claiming liens, for which he shall receive a fee of fifty cents from such person filing said claim. A copy of said notice shall be published, at the expense of the claimant, in some newspaper printed in said county, once in each week for four successive weeks after filing such notice with the register aforesaid. If, however, there shall be no paper published in said county, then the claimant of said lien shall post notices of his claim for four successive weeks, in four of the most public places in the township in which said improvement is situated, but it shall not be necessary to publish or post copies of any contract referred to in the last preceding section.

SEC. 4. The original contractor shall, as often as requested, in writing, by the owner or lessee, or his agent, make out and give to him a statement of the number of persons in his employ, and sub-contractors, giving their names and the rate of wages or terms of contract, and how much, if anything, is due to them, or any of them, which statement shall be made under oath, if required.

SEC. 5. If the money then due and payable to such person shall not be paid within ten days after service of said notice as aforesaid, or if such money shall not be so due and payable, then within ten days after the money shall become due and payable, and if the amount claimed by such person shall be admitted in writing to be due him by the contractor or sub-contractor by whom said money is directly payable, then such person may commence suit therefor in any court having jurisdiction of the amount claimed to be due against the owner or lessee, as if he were the original debtor, and judgment may be rendered, and execution had thereon, as in other cases. If the amount so claimed to be due shall not be admitted by the contractor or sub-contractor directly liable to pay the same, then within ten days after service of said notice as aforesaid, or within ten days after said money has become due and payable, the claimant may commence suit therefor before any court of competent jurisdiction, against the owner or lessee and the contractor directly liable to pay the same, jointly, and judgment may be rendered, and execution may be had thereon, as in other cases: *Provided however*, That when any judgment may be rendered against any owner or lessee, or against any owner or lessee and contractor, jointly, such owner or lessee may show to the court the amount actually due and payable from such owner or lessee to such contractor at the time said suit was commenced, and the court shall cause the amount so shown to be due to be entered upon the records thereof, and whenever execution shall issue for the collection of said judgment. the amount so shown to be due from said owner or lessee shall be endorsed on such execution, and no greater sum shall be collected of such owner or lessee than the amount so endorsed: *Provided further*, That when judgment shall be rendered against said owner or lessee upon any claim admitted in writing by any contractor as aforesaid, such owner or lessee shall be solely liable to pay the costs of said suit: *And also provided further*, No judgment against such owner or lessee shall be a bar to any suit brought for the amount of said claim, or any portion thereof remaining unpaid, against the contractor directly liable to pay the same to said claimant.

SEC. 6. Should the original contractor, for any cause, fail to complete his contract, any person entitled to a lien, as aforesaid, may file his petition in any court of record, against the owner or lessee and contractor, setting forth the nature of his claim, the amount due, as near as may be, and the names of the parties employed on such house, or other improvement, subject to liens; and notice of such suit shall be served on the persons therein named, and such as shall appear shall have their claims adjudicated, and decree shall be entered against the owner or lessee and original contractor, for so much as the work and material shall be shown to be reasonably worth, according to the original contract price, first deducting so much as shall have been rightfully paid on said original contract by the owner or lessee, the balance to be divided between such claimants in proportion to their respective interests, to be ascertained by the court, the premises to be sold within thirty days from the date of such decree, unless the judgment shall be sooner paid.

SEC. 7. No payments to the original contractor, or to any sub-contractor, by such owner or lessee, shall be regarded as rightfully made, if made in violation of the rights conferred by this act.

SEC. 8. The lien hereby created shall continue for six months from the time of the performance of the sub-contract, or doing of the work, or furnishing materials, as aforesaid, except where suit shall be commenced as aforesaid, and in such cases all liens shall be barred by decrees entered in said case.

Approved April 17, 1871.

CHAPTER LI.

DOMESTIC RELATIONS.

MARRIAGE — REGISTRATION OF BIRTHS, MARRIAGES, AND DEATHS — DIVORCE.

If otherwise competent, males eighteen years of age, and females sixteen years of age, are deemed capable in law of contracting marriage.

No man shall marry his mother, grandmother, daughter, grand-daughter, stepmother, grandfather's wife, son's wife, grandson's wife, wife's mother, wife's grandmother, wife's daughter, wife's grand-daughter, nor his sister, brother's daughter, sister's daughter, father's sister, or mother's sister.

No woman shall marry her father, grandfather, son, grandson, stepfather, grandmother's husband, daughter's husband, grand-daughter's husband, husband's father, husband's grandfather, husband's son, husband's grandson, nor her brother, brother's son, sister's son, father's brother, or mother's brother.

No marriage shall be contracted whilst either party has a former wife or husband living, unless the marriage of such former wife or husband shall have been dissolved.

No white person shall intermarry with a negro.

Marriages may be solemnized by Justices of the Peace and Ministers of the Gospel; or, so far as relates to the manner, may be solemnized according to the usages of any society or denomination.

All Justices of the Peace and Ministers of the Gospel are required, before solemnizing any marriage, to examine at least one of the parties under oath, touching the legality of such intended marriage.

All marriages must be solemnized in the presence of at least two witnesses besides the Minister or Magistrate.

Persons authorized to solemnize marriages (Ministers of the Gospel and Justices of the Peace) are required to make a record of each marriage solemnized by them; and the keeper of the records of the meetings in which any marriage among the Friends or Quakers shall be solemnized, shall make a record of such marriage.

Certificates of marriage shall be .furnished by the Minister, Justice, or Clerk, to either of the parties to such marriage. Certified copies of the record of marriages must be sent to the County Clerk, who is required to record the same.

It is the duty of the Supervisor of each township, and the Supervisor or Assessor of any city or ward therein, to return to the County Clerk, on or before the first day of June, in each year, a statement of the births and deaths which have occurred in their respective townships, cities, and wards during the year ending on the last day of the preceding December. But in the city of Detroit, persons are appointed by the Common Council to perform this duty.

Divorce.—All marriages prohibited by law on account of the relationship of the parties, or on account of either of them having a former wife or husband living; all marriages solemnized while either party was an idiot or insane; all marriages between a white person and a negro, if solemnized within this State; all marriages solemnized when either party was under the age of legal consent, if they shall separate during such nonage, and not live together afterwards, or in case the consent of one of the parties was obtained by force or fraud, and there shall have been no subsequent voluntary *cohabitation* of the parties, shall be deemed void without any decree of divorce.

A sentence to imprisonment for life, of either party, dissolves the marriage, without any decree of divorce.

[For grounds for granting a divorce, see note to this chapter.]

During the pending of a suit for divorce, the Court has power to make such order concerning the care and custody of the *minor* children and for the support of the wife by the husband as shall seem suitable and proper; and when a decree is granted, the Court makes such order as to the future care of the children and support of the wife as shall appear just and proper under all the circumstances.

When the marriage is dissolved, on account of the imprisonment of the husband, adultery by the husband, misconduct, or habitual drunkenness of the husband, the wife shall be entitled to her dower in his lands, the same as if he were dead.

The Court has power to grant a divorce from bed and board, without dissolving the marriage, in cases where the ground of complaint is extreme cruelty, or the neglect of the husband to support the wife.

Questions — At what age may parties contract marriage? Who shall not *intermarry?* Who may solemnize marriages? What examination is required? How many witnesses are required? What is said of certificates and records of marriages? What is required of Supervisors and Assessors with reference to statements of births and deaths? What is said of the care and support of minor children, and of the wife, in divorce cases? For what cause may a divorce from bed and board only, be granted?

NOTE.- -The following are recognized by our statute as grounds for granting a divorce, to the aggrieved party: Adultery; physical incompetency; sentence of one of the parties to imprisonment for three years or more; when either party shall desert the other for a term of two years; when either party shall have become an habitual drunkard. And the Court may, in its discretion, grant a decree of divorce for the cause of extreme cruelty, or, on the complaint of the wife, where the husband neglects or refuses to support her, being able to furnish such support. The Court will not grant a divorce to a party who is shown to be guilty of the same crime or misconduct charged against the defendant.

CHAPTER LII.

OF THE DOMESTIC RELATIONS, CONTINUED — HUSBAND AND WIFE — RIGHTS OF MARRIED WOMEN.

It is the duty of the husband to maintain and support his wife; and in case he abandon her and leave the State without sufficient provision for her support, the Probate Court may authorize her to sell his personal property, and collect moneys or other property due and belonging to him, and to use the same as her own.

A married woman may dispose of her property the same as if she were unmarried, and may make and enforce contracts for the purchase or sale of property. Her property is not liable for the debts of her husband. She may sue and be sued, in relation to her separate property, without joining her husband in such suit; and may carry on business in her own name.

While the husband is liable for the support of his wife, that is, for necessaries furnished her, he is not liable upon her contracts for other things.

The wife may mortgage her property to secure a debt of her own, or that of another person, but a note signed by her as surety, cannot be enforced against her. She may, however, buy goods for use in her husband's family, and be liable therefor, provided the goods were purchased with the understanding that she should pay for them. She may insure her life for the benefit of her husband, or her husband's life for her own benefit.

A mortgage, given by the husband, upon the homestead, or other property exempt by law from sale or execution, is *invalid* unless signed by the wife.

Where property of the husband has been taken from him on a mortgage, invalid for want of her signature, or upon an execution, where the property was not subject to levy, the wife may bring suit to recover the same, in her own name.

The widow of every deceased person is entitled to dower, or the use, during her natural life, of one-third part of all the lands whereof her husband was *seized* of an *estate of inheritance*, at any time during the marriage, unless she has conveyed the same away, or unless she has entered into an agreement to accept a certain consideration in *lieu* of dower.

Provision is made by law, for an allowance out of the husband's personal estate for the support of the widow and children, until such estate can be settled.

Questions—What is required of a married man as to the support of his wife? In case he abandons her, what provision is made by law as to her support? What rights has a married woman concerning property and the making of contracts? With reference to suits? For what is the husband not liable? What is said of her right to be surety for another? Of her liability for goods furnished to her for the family? Of her right to insure the life of herself or husband? What mortgages are invalid without her signature? What property of her husband may she recover by suit? What is said of dower? Of an allowance out of the personal property of a deceased husband?

CHAPTER LIII.

THE INTERNAL POLICE OF THE STATE.

OF DISORDERLY PERSONS — WHO REQUIRED TO GIVE SECURITY FOR GOOD BEHAVIOR.

All persons who run away, or threaten to run away, who,. being of sufficient ability, refuse or neglect to support their families, or leave their wives or children a burden on the public; all persons pretending to tell fortunes, or where or with whom lost or stolen goods may be found ; all common prostitutes ; all keepers of bawdy houses, or houses for the resort of prostitutes ; all drunkards, tipplers, gamesters, or other disorderly persons ; all persons who have no visible calling or business to maintain themselves by, or who do, for the most part, support themselves by gaming ; all *jugglers*, common showmen, and *mountebanks*, who exhibit or perform for profit, any *puppet shows*, wire or rope dancing, or other idle shows, acts or feats ; all persons who keep in any highway, or any public place, any gaming table, wheel of fortune, box, machine, instrument, or device for the purpose of gaming; all persons who go about with such table, wheel of fortune, box, machine, instrument, or device, exhibiting tricks or gaming therewith; all persons who play in the public streets or highways, with cards, dice, or any instrument or device for gaming ; and all *vagrants* shall be deemed disorderly persons, and may be required to furnish security for their good behavior, for not less than sixty-five days, nor more than one year thereafter; and in case of failure to furnish such security, shall be *committed* to jail, until discharged according to law. Such persons may be discharged from confinement on furnishing the security required; or, the Circuit Court may discharge such person if, in the judgment of the Court, the circumstances of the case warrant it, without such security; or may authorize the Superintendents of the Poor to *bind out*, as servants or *apprentices*, such disorderly persons as are under twenty-one years of age, until they reach the age of twenty-one years. The Circuit Court may also order disorderly persons to be kept at hard labor for any time not exceeding six months.

Questions—Who are deemed disorderly persons? What may be required of them? In case of a failure to furnish security for good behavior, what may be done with them? What authority has the Circuit Court in such cases?

CHAPTER LIV.

OF THE OBSERVANCE OF THE SABBATH — GAMING AND THE PENALTIES THEREFOR.

The law provides that any person who, on the first day of the week, shall engage in any business or labor, except works of necessity or charity, or who shall attend any dancing or at any public *diversion*, show or entertainment, or take part in any sport, game or play, shall be punished by a fine of not exceeding ten dollars, for each offense.

Hotel-keepers shall not, under a penalty of five dollars, permit persons, other than their *guests*, to remain upon their premises on the Sabbath.

No civil suits can be commenced, nor can courts be held on the Sabbath.

Persons who intentionally interrupt or disturb any assembly of people met for the purpose of worshiping God, shall be punished by a fine of not less than two nor more than fifty dollars, or by imprisonment in the county jail not exceeding thirty days.

Agreements made on the Sabbath are *void*. Persons who *conscientiously* believe that the seventh day of the week (Saturday) ought to be observed as the Sabbath, and actually *refrain* from *secular* business and labor on that day, shall not be liable to the penalties prescribed for performing secular business or labor on the first day of the week, provided they disturb no other persons.

Gaming.—If any person, by playing at any game of chance, or by betting, lose to any person so betting or playing, any money or goods, he may *recover* the same, or the value thereof, in an action for that purpose. If the person losing the money or goods does not, within three months after his loss, sue for the same, the winner is subject to a fine not exceeding three times the value of the money or goods lost.

If any person shall win or lose at any time or sitting, by gaming or betting on the hands or sides of such as are gaming, any money or goods of the value of five dollars or more, whether the same be paid over or not, shall forfeit and pay three times the value of such money or goods. All notes, bonds, mortgages or conveyances in which the consideration, in whole or in part, is for money or goods won by gaming or betting, are void, except as to those who hold or claim under them in good faith, and without notice of the illegality of such contract or conveyance.

Persons who keep, or knowingly permit to be kept, in any house, building, yard or garden which he occupies, any table for the purpose of playing at billiards for hire, gain or reward, or permit persons to *resort* to such place for the purpose of playing at billiards, nine-pins or other like game, cards or dice, or any other unlawful game, shall forfeit a sum not exceeding one hundred dollars, and give security that he will not be guilty of any offense against the chapter of the statute to compel the observance of the Sabbath and to prevent gaming.

Persons playing at such games, at such tables or alleys, thereby forfeit a sum not less than two nor more than ten dollars for each offense.

Questions — What acts are prohibited on the first day of the week? What is said of hotel keepers? What of agreements made on the Sabbath? What exception as to labor on the Sabbath is made? In case money or goods shall be lost by playing at games of chance or betting, how may the same be recovered? How and under what circumstances may the winner or loser be punished? What is said of the validity of securities or conveyances given for moneys or goods won by betting or at games of chance?

CHAPTER LV.

THE LAW OF THE ROAD — CONDUCT OF DRIVERS — DESTRUC-
TION OF TIMBER MARKS.

Whenever persons, traveling with a team, meet each
other on any road or bridge, each person is required to drive
to the right of the middle of the traveled part of the road or
bridge. A failure to do this, subjects the person so failing,
to a penalty not exceeding twenty dollars, and to the payment
of whatever damages a party may sustain by reason of such
failure.

No hack or stage proprietor is allowed to keep a driver
who is in the habit of using intoxicating liquors to excess;
and for so doing he is liable to a penalty of five dollars a day
for the time he retains him in his service.

If such driver is intoxicated while driving a coach, stage,
hack or omnibus, it is the duty of the proprietor to discharge
him as soon as notified of the fact by any passenger, under
oath, and in writing, who witnessed the same; and a failure to
discharge such driver, subjects the proprietor to a penalty of
five dollars per day so long as he shall keep him.

If a driver of a carriage for the conveyance of passen-
gers for hire, intentionally causes or permits his horses to run
away, whether any person be in the carriage or not, he is
liable to a fine not exceeding one hundred dollars, or imprisonment in the county jail not exceeding thirty days, or both,
at the discretion of the Court. If such driver shall leave his
horses while attached to a carriage in or on which any passenger may be at the time, without some suitable person to take

charge of them, he shall forfeit a sum not exceeding twenty dollars.

Proprietors of public conveyances are liable to persons injured, for the misconduct of the driver, while in the employment of such proprietor.

Destruction of Timber Marks. — Whoever shall unlaw-fully cut out, alter, or destroy any mark of the owner, made on any logs, timber or lumber, put into any lake, stream, or pond, shall forfeit a sum not exceeding ten dollars, for each log, stick of timber, or piece of lumber, the mark of which he shall have so altered, cut or destroyed, and shall be liable to the party injured in three times the amount of the damage.

Whoever takes, without the consent of the owner, logs, timber, boards, or planks, floating in any of the waters of this State, or lying on the banks or shores, or on any island on which they shall have drifted, is liable to the owner in three times the amount of the damages; but if they shall have remained there for two years, without the owner's having paid the owner of the land, or offered to pay him the damages occasioned by reason of their lying on his land, and whatever damages he would sustain by their removal, they become the property of the land-owner.

Questions — What does the law require of persons driving teams on the highways, when meeting each other? What is the penalty for stage proprietors retaining in their employ intemperate drivers? What is said with reference to hitching or fastening horses attached to public conveyances? Who are liable for injuries occasioned by misconduct of drivers? What is said of the destruction of certain timber marks? What is said with reference to logs, timber and lumber that may float upon the lands of any person?

CHAPTER LVI.

LOST GOODS AND STRAY BEASTS.

Any person finding lost goods is required immediately to give notice to the owner, if known. If not, and the goods are worth three dollars or more, he must, within two days, post notices in two public places within the township where the property was found, and within seven days give written notice to the Town Clerk, and pay him twenty-five cents for making an entry thereof in a book kept for that purpose.

If the value of the goods be ten dollars or more, notice must also be published within a month, in a newspaper of the county, if there be one, and if not, then in a newspaper of an adjoining county, for six weeks.

Any *resident freeholder* of any township, may take up any stray horses, mules, or asses, going at large beyond the range where they usually run at large ; and may also take up, between the months of November and March, stray cattle, sheep, or swine.

Such finder is required to give immediate notice to the owner, if known. He must, within ten days, have notice thereof entered in the Township Clerk's book, giving the color, age and marks of the animals, as near as may be, together with the name and place of residence of the finder, and pay the Clerk fifty cents. The Clerk sends a copy of the notice to the County Clerk.

If the owner does not appear within one month, and claim his property, and the animals taken up shall be worth more than ten dollars, the finder is required to advertise as in case of lost goods.

9

The finder of lost goods or stray animals, of the value of ten dollars or more, must, within three months, procure an appraisal of the property to be made, and certified by a Justice of the Peace, which shall be filed with the Clerk.

If the owner of lost goods at any time within one year, claims his property, he is *entitled* to it, or its value, on paying all costs and charges, together with a reasonable *compensation* to the finder for keeping and taking care of it, and for his traveling expenses, to be determined by a Justice of the Peace, if the parties fail to agree.

If no owner appears, in one year, the lost money or goods shall belong to the finder, he paying one-half their value to the Township Treasurer.

If the owner of such stray beasts appears in six months, and pays all lawful charges, he is entitled to them ; but if not, they must be sold at auction by a constable, he first giving notice thereof in writing, by posting the same in three public places in the township, and the moneys realized, after paying costs and charges, is to be deposited in the treasury of the township.

If the owner appears within one year after the entry of the notice with the Town Clerk, he is entitled to the money deposited with the Treasurer, but if he shall not so appear, the money belongs to the township.

If the person finding property or taking up strays shall fail to give the required notices, and shall fraudulently *appropriate* the property to his own use, he is subject to a penalty of not less than ten nor more than fifty dollars, and to be imprisoned in the county jail until the fine be paid, not exceeding ninety days.

If a person shall unlawfully take away any animal taken up as a stray, without having first paid the charges, he is liable to the finder for the full value of the property.

Questions —What is the duty of persons finding lost goods? What is his duty if the goods exceed in value three dollars? Where they exceed ten dollars? Who may take up stray beasts? When may cattle, sheep, and swine be taken up? What is required of the finder of stray animals? When may the owner of lost goods *reclaim* them? On what terms? If the owner does not appear, to whom does the property belong? How and when may the owner of stray beasts reclaim them? If the owner does not appear in six months, what is done with stray animals? What is done with the money? When and how may the owner procure the money deposited with the Treasurer? If the owner fails to appear within one year, to whom does the money belong? What is the penalty where the finder of goods appropriates them to his own use, fraudulently, without giving the required notice? In case a person takes away an animal taken up as a stray, without having first paid the charges, what is his liability?

· CHAPTER LVII.

RUNNING AT LARGE OF ANIMALS — UNCLAIMED PROPERTY — THEATRICAL EXHIBITIONS AND SHOWS — GUNPOWDER — DOGS — SHEEP.

By a law passed in 1867, the Board of Supervisors of any county may pass a resolution prohibiting the running at large of horses, cattle, sheep and swine. In those counties where such resolution has been passed, it is lawful for any person to seize and take into his possession any animal which may be trespassing upon his premises, or which may be in any public highway, and opposite the land owned or occupied by him, contrary to such resolution. The person making such seizure is required to notify a Justice of the Peace or Highway Commissioner of the fact. The officer thus notified posts notices advertising the public sale of such animals in sixty days.

After paying the costs and charges, the surplus moneys arising from the sale are kept for the owner, and if he calls for them within one year, they are paid over to him ; if not, they belong to the township. If the owner so desires, he may *redeem* the animal at any time within a year after the sale, by paying all costs and charges, and a reasonable *compensation* for keeping such animal.

At any time before the sale of the animal, the owner may have the possession of such animal, on paying the costs and charges provided for by law.

The owner of any bull, stallion, boar, or ram, is subject to a fine of five dollars for allowing such animals to run at large.

Unclaimed Property. — Whenever personal property is sent to, or left with warehouse-keepers, or to the keeper of any depot, it is the duty of the person receiving and having charge of the same, to enter in a book the description and time of receiving such goods.

If such goods were not left to be forwarded or otherwise disposed of, according to directions, the person having them in charge is required to notify the owner, if his residence be known, by letter.

In case such property is not claimed in three months, it is advertised for four weeks, the notice stating that unless such property shall be claimed within three months from the first publication of such notice, and the lawful charges paid, they will be sold. If not claimed, a Justice of the Peace orders a Constable to sell the goods. The Constable, after making the sale, returns the money to the Justice, who pays the charges and expenses of the sale, and pays over to the County Treasurer the *surplus* moneys, where the person whose goods were sold may get them at any time within five years.

If not claimed in five years, the County Treasurer pays them over into the State Treasury for the use of the State.

Theatrical Exhibitions and Shows.—Township or village boards have authority to *license* theatrical exhibitions, public shows, and such other exhibitions as they deem proper, to which admission is obtained on payment of money, upon such terms and conditions as they shall think reasonable, and may regulate the same as they shall think necessary for the preservation of order.

Any person who shall set up or promote any such exhibition or show without a license, or contrary to the terms of such a license, may be fined a sum not exceeding two hundred dollars.

Gunpowder.—The inhabitants of incorporated villages or townships, at any regular meeting, may, by *resolution*, order that no gunpowder shall be kept in the township or village, unless in tight casks or canisters; and that not over fifty pounds shall be kept in any building, ship or vessel, within twenty-five rods of any other building or wharf; not over twenty-five pounds within ten rods of any other building; and that not over one pound shall be kept in any building within ten rods of any other building, unless it be secured in copper, tin, or brass canisters, holding not exceeding five pounds each, and closely covered with copper, brass, or tin covers. A violation of this provision subjects the offender to a fine not exceeding twenty dollars; but the law is not designed to apply to the manufacturer of powder, nor to prevent carrying it through the township.

Dog Licenses.—The Legislature of 1873, passed an act to provide for the *licensing* and keeping of dogs. By this act, the owner or keeper of every male dog must pay to the City or Township Clerk a license of one dollar; for every female dog, three dollars. These licenses run until the first of April next following their date. During the continuance of the license, the owner is required to keep a collar on the dog's neck, distinctly marked with the owner's name.

The moneys raised from licenses constitute a fund for the payment of damages which persons may sustain by the killing or wounding of sheep or lambs, by dogs.

Whoever keeps a dog without a license and collar is subject to a forfeiture of ten dollars.

It is the duty of Constables and Policemen to kill all dogs found not licensed and collared.

From this, it would seem that dogs are not " entitled to life, liberty, and the pursuit of happiness," unless they happen to belong to some one able to license and collar them.

Sheep. — Any person who shall knowingly bring into this State, sheep having any *contagious* disease, is subject to a penalty of not less than fifty dollars, and on failure to pay the same, may be imprisoned in the county jail not exceeding three months ; and any person who shall allow his sheep to run at large, on the highway, knowing them to have a contagious disease, is subject to a penalty of not less than fifty nor more than one hundred dollars ; and in default of payment may be imprisoned in the County Jail not to exceed three months.

Questions — In those counties where cattle, horses, sheep and swine are prohibited from running at large, what provision is made for seizing such animals when at large? What proceedings are had to effect a sale of such animals? What is done with the proceeds of the sale? May the owner redeem the animals when sold? On what terms may the owner procure the possession of animals seized, for running at large contrary to law? What are warehousemen and other *bailees* required to do in regard to property consigned to them? Under what circumstances may such goods be sold? How are such sales effected? What disposition is made of the moneys arising from the sale? What powers have township and village boards with reference to theatrical exhibitions and shows? What is the penalty for setting up or promoting such shows or exhibitions without a license, or contrary to the terms of such license? What regulations may the inhabitants of townships and villages make concerning the keeping of gunpowder? What can you say in reference to the dog-license law? What is the penalty for importing diseased sheep? For allowing such sheep to run at large in the highways?

CHAPTER LVIII.

LAWS FOR .THE PROTECTION OF FISH.

It is unlawful to put into any of the waters of the State, where fish are taken, any *offal*, blood, putrid brine, putrid fish, or filth of any description. The penalty for a violation of this law, is a fine not exceeding three hundred dollars, or imprisonment not exceeding thirty days, or both, at the discretion of the Court.

All fish, offal, or filth accruing from the catching and curing of fish, must be burned or buried ten rods distant from the beach or shore of the river or lake.

The *spawn* taken from all whitefish caught shall be forthwith deposited in the waters near the spawning places from which the fish were taken.

For a violation of the provisions of law mentioned in either of the last two paragraphs, the offender is subject to a penalty of not more than one hundred dollars, nor less than twenty-five dollars and costs, or to imprisonment in the County Jail for a period not exceeding thirty days, or both, at the discretion of the Court.

The Boards of Supervisors of the several counties have the power to make rules and regulations for fishing with nets and all manner of fishing tackle, in those counties where the law does not, by express terms or by reasonable implication, deprive them of this power.

The Boards, except in those counties referred to in the preceding paragraphs, and to which reference will be made hereafter, are authorized and required to grant, on the application of any *transient* or *non-resident* person or persons, a written permission or license for one year, for each and every pound or trap net used, on payment of fifty dollars.

A law was passed in 1867, to prevent fishing with seines and every kind of continuous nets, in the waters of the counties of Branch, Livingston, Cass, St. Joseph, Kent, Ionia, Genesee, and Calhoun, or in any of the lakes, rivers, or streams of Macomb county, under a penalty of not more than one hundred dollars, or imprisonment in the County Jail not more than sixty days, to be determined by the Court. A similar act was passed in 1865 with reference to fishing in the counties of Jackson, Hillsdale, Washtenaw, Van Buren, Calhoun, Kalamazoo, Barry, Eaton, and the townships of Rollin, Medina, Seneca, Dover, Hudson, Cambridge, Franklin, and Woodstock, in Lenawee county. At the same session of the Legislature, an act similar to the foregoing was passed, applying to all the inland lakes or small streams of all the territory of the State, according to the United States survey, north of the township line numbered twenty, north.

The law makes it the duty of the owners or occupants of mill-dams to construct proper *shutes*, to admit the passage of fish during the months of April, May, and June. A failure to do this subjects the person in *default* to a fine not exceeding one hundred dollars, or imprisonment in the County Jail not exceeding ninety days.

It is unlawful for any person to place a *weir dam*, *fish weir*, or weir net, across any race, drain, stream, or inland river of this State, so as to obstruct the free passage of fish up and down the same; and the offender is subject to a fine of not less than five nor more than fifty dollars, for each offense, and also to the payment of two dollars additional penalty for every day he shall continue to keep up such fish weir or weir net, after having been notified by any elector of the township wherein such fish weir or weir net may be, feeling himself aggrieved thereby, to remove the same.

By the provisions of an act passed in 1873, it is unlawful to kill at any time, by means of nets, traps, or seines, in any inland lake, river, or stream, or by any other means between the first day of October and the first day of April next succeeding, any speckled trout or grayling. The penalty for a violation of this provision is a fine not exceeding one hundred dollars, nor less than twenty-five dollars, or imprisonment in the County Jail not exceeding thirty days, or both, at the discretion of the Court. At the same session an act was passed, providing "that it shall not be lawful hereafter, at any time, to fish with seines, trap-nets, pound-nets, dip-nets, or any species of continuous nets, or during the months of March, April, May and June by spearing or shooting, in any of the waters of the State of Michigan, except Lakes Michigan, Superior, Huron, St. Clair, the St. Clair and Detroit rivers, and Lake Erie: *Provided*, Nothing in this act shall be construed as prohibiting sole owners of fish ponds from fishing therein, as they may think proper."

In 1873, the Legislature passed an act to establish a Board of Commissioners to increase the product of the fisheries. This Board is required to locate a State fish-breeding establishment, for the *artificial propagation* and cultivation of whitefish, and such other kinds of the better class of food fishes as they may direct. The duties of this Board have been referred to in a preceding chapter.

Questions—What materials shall not be put into the waters of this State, where fish are taken? What is the penalty for violating this provision? What must be done with offal, etc, which accrues from the catching and curing of fish? What must be done with the spawn, in certain cases? What is the penalty for refusing or neglecting to dispose of the offal, etc., and of the spawn, as directed? What powers have Boards of Supervisors in relation to fishing? What is said of the law of 1867? Of the acts of 1865? What is said of the construction of shutes? Of weir dams and weir nets? Of the several acts of 1873? What is said of the act of 1873, with reference to a Board of Fish Commissioners?

CHAPTER LIX.

OF THE PROTECTION OF GAME, SONG BIRDS, AND MUSK-RATS.

It is provided by law that no person or persons shall pursue, or hunt, or kill any wild elk, wild buck, doe, or fawn, save only during the months of October, November, and December in each year; or kill or destroy by any means whatever, or attempt to take or destroy any wild turkey at any time during the year, except in the months of September, October, November, and December in each year; or kill or destroy, by any means whatever, any woodcock until after the fifth of July; or any prairie chicken, or pinnated grouse, ruffled grouse, commonly called partridge or pheasant, or any wood duck, teal duck, or mallard duck, save only from the first day of September in each year to the first day of January next following

It is also provided that no person or persons shall kill or

·destroy, or attempt to kill or destroy, any quail, sometimes called Virginia partridge, except during the months of October, November, and December in each year.

The law also provides that no person shall kill, or attempt to kill, any wild duck, or other wild fowl, with or by means of a *swivel* or *punt* gun, or rob or destroy the nests of any wild duck or wild geese, or in any manner kill or molest the same while they are sitting at night on their nesting places.

No person shall sell, or expose for sale, any of the birds or animals protected by this act, after the expiration of thirty days next succeeding the times limited and prescribed for the killing of any such birds or animals : *Provided however*, That it shall be lawful to expose for sale, and to sell, any live quail for the purpose of preserving the same alive through the winter.

Any person violating any of the foregoing provisions, is deemed guilty of a *misdemeanor*, and is liable to a penalty of fifty dollars for each offense, and on conviction thereof, is to be committed to the common jail until such penalty is paid; *provided*, that the imprisonment shall not exceed thirty days.

All persons within this State are prohibited from killing any robin, night-hawk, whippoorwill, finch, thrush, lark, sparrow, cherry-bird, swallow, yellow-bird, blue-bird, brown-thrasher, wren, mattin, oriole, wood-pecker, bobolink, or any song bird, and from robbing the nests of such birds, under a penalty of five dollars for each bird so killed, and for each nest robbed.

Any person or company having any of the above named birds or animals in their possession for transportation, or who shall transport the same, after the expiration of thirty days next succeeding the times limited and prescribed for the killing of such birds or animals, is liable to be punished by a fine not less than ten dollars, nor more than one hundred dollars.

This penalty, however, does not apply to the transportation of quails which are to be kept alive during the winter, nor to the transportation of such birds or animals *in transitu* through this State from other States, where it is lawful to kill them at the time of such transportation.

All persons are prohibited from using guns or other firearms, to maim, kill, or destroy any wild pigeon or pigeons at or within one half mile of the place or places where they are gathered in bodies for the purpose of brooding their young, known as pigeon nestings; and no person shall in any way maim, kill, or destroy any wild pigeon or pigeons within their roostings any where within the limits of this State; and any person who shall violate the law in this particular, is subject to a penalty of fifty dollars, with costs of suit.

Any person violating any of the provisions of this act, may be prosecuted before any Justice of the Peace of the county in which such violation is alleged to have taken place, or before any Court of competent jurisdiction; and it is made the duty of all Prosecuting Attorneys in this State to see that the provisions of this act are enforced in their respective counties, and to prosecute all offenders, on receiving information of the violation of any of the provisions of this act; and it is made the duty of Sheriffs, Under-Sheriffs, Deputy-Sheriffs, Constables, and Police officers, to inform against and prosecute all persons, whom there is probable cause to believe are guilty of violating any of the provisions of this act.

These provisions do not apply to any person who shall kill any of the birds or animals named, for the sole purpose of preserving them as specimens for scientific purposes, nor to any person who shall collect the eggs or nests of any bird for such scientific purposes. The prosecution in any such case is not required to prove that the killing of the bird or animal, or the taking of the nest or eggs, as the case may be, was not done for scientific purposes.

All prosecutions under this act must be brought within three months from the time the offense was committed.

The statute also provides against the destruction of musk-rats and musk-rat houses in the marshes, along the shores of Lakes Erie, St. Clair, Huron, and Michigan, or in or on the banks of any bayous or creeks tributary thereto, between the fifteenth day of April and the first day of January, under a penalty of three dollars for each musk-rat so killed or destroyed.

Penalties for the violation of this act may be sued for in the name of the people of the State of Michigan, before any Justice of the Peace in the county where the alleged offense was committed, and such suit shall be carried on in the same manner as prosecutions for other misdemeanors. Penalties are to be paid into the treasury of the county where the offense was committed, for the support of the township libraries of the county.

It is provided that this act shall not be so construed as to prevent the catching and killing of any animals specified in the foregoing sections, where there is danger of their doing injury to property, either public or private.

Questions — What is said, in the first paragraph of this lesson, of the killing, pursuing, or hunting of certain animals? During what months may these animals be killed? What is said of the killing of birds? What name is sometimes given to the quail? During what months may these be killed? Why this provision? What is meant by a swivel or punt gun? What is said of the sale of these birds or animals? What exception is made in respect to the sale of these birds or animals, and why? What penalty is attached to the violation of this act? What song birds may not be killed? Is the penalty the same for robbing nests as killing birds? What is said of transporting birds?

What is the penalty for violating this act? What exception to this penalty? What is said of killing or destroying pigeons? What are the places called where pigeons brood? What is the penalty for killing these birds or destroying their nests? What is the duty of the Prosecuting Attorney in this matter? What is the duty of other officers relative to such prosecutions? To whom do these provisions not apply? What is the prosecution not required to prove? Within what time must prosecutions be brought under this act? What is the law relative to the destruction of musk-rats? To what portions of the State does this act apply? State the penalty for its violation. How are such penalties secured? To what are such penalties applied? State the exceptions to the provisions of this act.

CHAPTER LX.

TRESPASS UPON CRANBERRY MARSHES — CANADA THISTLES, DESTRUCTION OF.

It is unlawful to enter upon the premises of another, without permission, to take and carry away cranberries or cranberry vines, or to injure them in any way. To do so, subjects the offender to imprisonment in the County Jail, not less than five days, or to a fine of not less than five dollars, or both, in the discretion of the Court; and if the offense is committed on the Sabbath, or in the night time, or while the offender is disguised, the fine is not less than ten dollars, and the imprisonment not less than ten days, or both, at the discretion of the Court; and any such person is also liable to the owner or occupant of the premises, in three times the amount of the actual damages.

Canada Thistles.—The owner or occupant of lands is required, under a penalty of ten dollars, to cut down and destroy all Canada thistles growing upon such land, or upon the highway running through or by such land, so often as shall be necessary to prevent them from going to seed.

Overseers of Highways and Highway Commissioners are required to cause all such thistles to be destroyed within their respective townships and districts.

Any person who shall knowingly sell any grass or other seed, among which there is any seed of the Canada thistle, shall be liable to a fine of twenty dollars.

Questions — What is said in relation to trespasses upon cranberry marshes? What circumstances are considered as an aggravation of the offense? What are the owners or occupants of lands required to do with reference to Canada thistles? What officers are to attend to the destruction of Canada thistles? What is the penalty for selling seeds containing seed of the Canada thistle?

CHAPTER LXI.

INTOXICATING LIQUORS — MANUFACTURE AND SALE OF, PRO-
HIBITED.

It is unlawful for any one to manufacture or sell, in person, or by his clerk or agent, spirituous or intoxicating liquors, except as provided by law.

It is not unlawful to manufacture alcohol containing not less than eighty parts in the hundred of pure alcohol. Druggists, who have given bonds, as the law requires, not to sell any spirituous or intoxicating liquors, or any mixed liquor, a part of which is spirituous or intoxicating, except to be used as a medicine, as a chemical agent in scientific, mechanical or manufacturing purposes, or wine for sacramental purposes; nor to sell the same to any person whom he knows, or has good reason to believe, intends to use it as a beverage, or to any person to be drank, for any purpose, upon the premises; nor to minors, unless upon the written order of his father, mother, guardian, or family physician, may sell such liquors according to the conditions and subject to the limitations of such bonds.

Manufacturers of alcohol manufactured in accordance with the provisions of law, may sell such alcohol to persons who have given such bonds as are mentioned above.

It is not unlawful to make cider from apples, or wine from grapes or other fruits grown or gathered by the manufacturer thereof, or to make beer, in this State, and free from all other intoxicating liquors; but in no case shall such beer be sold in less quantity than five gallons, or such wine or cider be sold in less quantity than one gallon, and sold to be, and be all taken away at one time; and all sales of such beer, in less quantities than five gallons, or of such wine or cider, in less quantity than one gallon, to be drank or used on the premises, shall be an unlawful sale.

It is not unlawful to sell liquors that are of foreign production, and which have been imported under the laws of the United States, and in accordance therewith, and contained in the original packages in which they were imported, and in quantities not less than the laws of the United States prescribe.

All payments for liquors sold in violation of law may be recovered back, by the person paying the same, his wife or any of his children, or his parent, guardian, husband, or employer; and all sales, notes, securities, or the like, made or given where the consideration thereof, either in whole or in part, shall have been the sale or agreement to sell liquor, contrary to law, shall be *void*, against all persons, and in all cases, except only as against the holders of *negotiable* securities, or the purchasers of property who may have paid therefor a fair price, and received the same upon a valuable and fair consideration, without notice or knowledge of such illegal consideration.

Where a person, by reason of intoxication, inflicts an injury upon the person or property of another, the injured party may recover his damages against the person furnishing the liquor that may have caused or contributed to the intoxication of such intoxicated person. And the owner or lessee of buildings having knowledge that intoxicating liquors are to be sold therein at retail as a beverage, are equally liable with the seller for damages resulting from such sales.

The giving away of intoxicating liquors, or any other shift or device, with intent to evade the law, shall be deemed an unlawful selling, and every person who, as clerk, agent or servant of another, shall sell any such liquor, shall be deemed equally guilty as his principal.

If any person shall knowingly solicit or encourage any person, who has previously used intoxicating drinks *habitually* or injuriously, to use as a *beverage* any such liquors, or if he shall voluntarily, directly or indirectly, give any such liquors, or cause the same to be given to such person, or shall, with the intention of having such person drink or use them, place any such liquors, or cause or procure the same to be placed where such person may obtain them, to be used as a beverage, such person so offending shall be subject to the penalties and forfeitures provided against selling such liquors.

The statute provides that persons found intoxicated may be compelled to appear before a Justice of the Peace, and disclose where and of whom he procured the liquors.

It is also provided that any person found drunk in a public place, may be fined five dollars.

The keeping or selling of liquors contrary to law, subjects the offender to a penalty of twenty-five dollars and costs; for the second offense, fifty dollars and costs; and for each subse-

10

quent offense, a fine of one hundred dollars and imprisonment in the County Jail, not less than three nor more than six months.

It is provided that common sellers and manufacturers of liquors in violation of law, shall, on each conviction, forfeit and pay double the amount specified in the last preceding section, with costs of suit or prosecution; and that for the third, or any subsequent conviction, shall, in addition to the forfeiture, be imprisoned for six months.

The law prohibits the employment of persons upon railroads who use intoxicating drinks as a bevergae, under a penalty of twenty-five dollars, where the officers of the company know that such employee uses such liquors as a beverage.

If any person shall bring into any jail any intoxicating liquors for sale or for the use of any prisoner, unless the same shall be certified to be absolutely necessary for the health of such prisoner, or if any officer or person employed in or about such jail shall knowingly permit any spirituous liquor to be sold or used in jail, contrary to law, such officer or person shall be subject to imprisonment not exceeding one year, or a fine not exceeding two hundred and fifty dollars, or both, in the discretion of the Court.

Questions — State what grade of alcohol may be lawfully manufactured. What is said as to the sale of liquors by druggists? What is said of the sale of alcohol by manufacturers? What is said of the manufacture of cider, wine and beer? What is said of the sale of these articles? What is said of liquors of foreign production? By whom may moneys paid out for liquors, in violation of law, be recovered? What of securities given for liquors? Who are liable for injuries inflicted by reason of intoxication? What is deemed equivalent to an unlawful sale of liquors? What is said of soliciting certain persons to use liquor as a beverage? What provision is made for procuring testimony as to where any intoxicated person procured his liquor? What is the penalty for being intoxicated in a public place?

What is the penalty for keeping or selling intoxicating liquors contrary to law? What is the punishment for being a common seller or manufacturer of liquors contrary to law? What is the law in regard to the employment of persons addicted to the use of intoxicating drinks, by railroad companies? What is said of the sale of intoxicating drinks in jails?

CHAPTER LXII.

OF CRIMES AND MISDEMEANORS.

TREASON — MURDER — DUELS — MANSLAUGHTER — MAIMING — ROBBERY — MALICIOUS THREATS — MARRIAGE UNDER DURESS OR BY FORCE — UNLAWFUL IMPRISONMENT — KIDNAPPING.

Persons accused of crime have the right to counsel and witnesses in open Court.

An *acquittal*, on a trial of the facts, is a *bar* to further prosecutions for the same offense.

Treason against the State, that is, *levying* war against it, or *adhering* to its enemies, giving them aid and comfort, is the highest crime known to our laws, and is punishable by death.

Murder in the first degree, that is, the *deliberate* and *premeditated* killing of a human being without cause, or the killing of a person while attempting to perpetrate any arson, rape, robbery, or burglary, subjects the offender to imprisonment for life in the State Prison. Murder in the second degree, that is, where the act of killing is done intentionally, but without that premeditation and deliberation which distinguish murder in the first degree, is punishable by imprisonment in the State Prison for life, or any number of years, in the discretion of the Court.

Fighting a duel, if death *ensue*, is murder in the first degree. Fighting a duel, although neither party be killed, or offering to fight one, subjects the offender to imprisonment in the State Prison not exceeding ten years, or to a fine not exceeding one thousand dollars and imprisonment in the County Jail not more than three years, and deprives the offender of the right to hold any office under the laws of this State. The penalties of the law against dueling apply to *seconds* as well as *principals*. Indeed, all who in any way encourage the fighting of a duel are subject to heavy penalties.

The crime of manslaughter, which consists in the killing of a human being, while under the influence of sudden *provo-cation*, or from heating of the blood, or stirring the passions to such an extent as to exclude the idea of *malice*, is punishable by imprisonment in the State Prison not more than fifteen years, or by fine not exceeding one thousand dollars.

Maiming or *disfiguring*, or attempting to maim or disfigure another, with malicious intent, or aiding in the commission of the offense, is punishable by imprisonment in the State Prison not more that ten years, or by fine not exceeding one thousand dollars, or both, at the discretion of the Court.

If a person *robs* another, such robber being armed with a dangerous weapon, with intent, if resisted, to kill or maim the person robbed, or if, being so armed, he shall wound or strike the person robbed, he shall be confined in the State Prison for life, or any number of years. If the robber be not armed, the punishment cannot exceed fifteen years' imprisonment.

If any person shall maliciously threaten to accuse another of any crime or offense, or to injure the person or property of another, with intent thereby to extort money or any pecuniary advantage, or with intent to compel the person so threatened to do any act against his will, he shall be punished by imprisonment in the State Prison, or in the County Jail, not exceeding two years, or by fine not exceeding one thousand dollars.

If any person shall take any woman unlawfully and against her will, and by force, *menace* or *duress*, compel her to marry him or any other person, he shall be punished by imprisonment in the State Prison for life or any term of years.

Imprisoning a person without lawful authority, or forcibly carrying such person out of the State, subjects the offender to imprisonment in the State Prison for a term not exceeding ten years, or to a fine not exceeding one thousand dollars.

The law against seduction, rape, and kindred crimes, is justly very severe, the penalty being imprisonment in the State Prison. To entice a girl under the age of sixteen years, away from father, mother, guardian, or other person having legal charge of her, for lustful or other base purposes, or for marriage, subjects the offender to imprisonment in the State Prison not exceeding three years, or to imprisonment in the County Jail not exceeding one year, or to a fine not exceeding one thousand dollars.

Questions — To what have persons accused of crime, a right? What is the effect of an acquittal? What is treason against the State? What is the penalty? Define murder, and state the penalty therefor. What is murder in the second degree? The penalty? What is said of dueling? Of challenges to fight duels? To what parties does the law against dueling apply? What is manslaughter? The punishment therefor? What is maiming? What is the penalty therefor? What is said of robbery? Of malicious threats? What is the penalty for compelling a woman to marry against her will? What is the penalty for unlawfully imprisoning or carrying a person out of the State?

CHAPTER LXIII.

OF CRIMES AND MISDEMEANORS, CONTINUED — ATTEMPTS TO
POISON — TAKING OR ENTICING CHILDREN AWAY FROM
PARENTS OR OTHERS — ABANDONMENT OF CHILDREN —
CARELESS USE OF FIRE-ARMS.

Mingling poison with food, drink or medicines ; to take
or to entice away any child under the age of twelve years,
with intent to detain or conceal such child from its parent,
guardian, or other person having the lawful charge of such
child, are crimes punishable by imprisonment in the State
Prison not more than ten years, or by imprisonment in the
County Jail not more than one year, or by fine not exceeding
one thousand dollars.

Any person having a child under six years of age in
charge, who shall expose such child in any street, field, town,
or other place, with intent to abandon it, he or she shall be
punished by imprisonment in the State Prison not more than
ten years.

Pointing a gun at another, intentionally, but without
malice, subjects the offender to a fine of not less than five nor
more than fifty dollars. If in such case the gun be discharged,
without injury, the offender is liable to a fine of not less than
one hundred dollars, or imprisonment in the County Jail not
to exceed one year, or both, at the discretion of the Court.
If death ensue from such discharge, the offense is deemed
manslaughter.

The statute makes provision for the punishment of persons who attempt to commit crime, even though they may fail

to accomplish their purpose ; and such punishment is graded according to the gravity of the crime attempted.

Questions—What is said with reference to mingling poison with food, drink, or medicine? Of enticing children away from parents or guardians? Of the careless use of fire-arms? Is there any punishment prescribed for attempting to commit crime?

CHAPTER LXIV.

OF OFFENSES AGAINST PROPERTY.

BURNING BUILDINGS AND OTHER PROPERTY — HOUSE-BREAK-ING, ETC. — LARCENY — RECEIVING STOLEN GOODS — EM-BEZZLEMENT.

Maliciously burning a dwelling-house of another in the night-time, if any person be lawfully within such house at the time, subjects the offender to imprisonment in the State Prison for life. If no person be in such house, or if the dwelling be burned in the day-time, the punishment is imprisonment for any term of years, to be fixed by the Court. Maliciously burning in the night-time, any meeting-house, church, court-house, college, academy, jail, railroad-depot, or other public building erected for public use ; or any banking-house, warehouse, store, manufactory, or mill of another, being, with the property therein contained, of the value of one thousand dollars, subjects the offender to imprisonment in the State Prison for any term of years. If the burning be in the day-time the imprisonment cannot exceed ten years.

It is unlawful to burn any bridge, *lock*, dam, or *flume*, or any ship, boat, or vessel of another, or to burn any wood, lumber, fences, grain, or other vegetable product of another, or to burn any property to defraud insurance companies ; and in all such cases appropriate penalties are attached to a violation of the law.

Breaking and entering a dwelling-house in the night-time, with the intent to commit any *felony* or *larceny*, is an offense, punishable by imprisonment in the State Prison not more than twenty years. If the burglar is armed and assaults a person being lawfully in such house, it is deemed an aggravation of the offense.

The breaking and entering of any dwelling-house, shop, store, railroad depot, warehouse, ship, boat, vessel, mill, school-house, or factory, with the intent to commit a felony or larceny, is deemed a State Prison offense, and when committed in the night-time the act is deemed more *heinous*.

Stealing from a dwelling or other building, or at a fire, or from the person of another, are deemed aggravated cases of larceny, and are punishable by imprisonment in the State Prison. Other cases of larceny, unless the value of the property stolen exceeds twenty-five dollars, are punishable by imprisonment in the County Jail, or by fine ; the penalty for a second, or any subsequent offense, being more severe.

The buying, receiving, or concealment, of stolen property, knowing it to have been stolen, subjects the offender to imprisonment in the State Prison not more than five years, or to a fine not exceeding five hundred dollars and imprisonment in the County Jail not more than one year.

Persons who, by virtue of their employment, come into possession of personal property, and appropriate it to their own use, are guilty of embezzlement, and may be punished by imprisonment in the State Prison, or by fine and imprisonment in the County Jail.

Questions—What is said of the burning of dwelling-houses in the night time? Of other buildings? Of the burning of bridges, locks, &c.? What is said of breaking into and entering a dwelling-house in the night time? Of breaking into other buildings? Mention certain aggravated cases of larceny. What is said of buying, receiving, or concealing stolen property? Of embezzlement?

CHAPTER LXV.

FALSE REPRESENTATIONS AND PRETENSES — DESTRUCTION AND FITTING OUT OF VESSELS, WITH MALICIOUS INTENT — MALICIOUS INJURIES — BURGLAR'S TOOLS — LARCENY IN OTHER STATES — INJURIES TO SHADE TREES — OF CERTAIN TRESPASSES.

Every person who shall falsely *personate* another, and thereby receive property with the intent to convert it to his own use, is guilty of larceny. Obtaining property under false pretenses, or *tokens*, is an offense punishable by imprisonment in the State Prison not exceeding ten years, or by fine not exceeding five hundred dollars, or imprisonment in the County Jail not exceeding one year.

The willful destruction of vessels, with intent to injure another, is punishable by imprisonment in the State Prison not more than fifteen years. Fitting out vessels, with intent that they shall be destroyed, or to defraud the owner or insurer; making a false invoice of cargo, with like intention; making, or procuring a false protest, with intent to injure or defraud any insurer, are deemed offenses, punishable by imprisonment in the State Prison, or by fine and imprisonment in the County Jail.

Malicious injuries to beasts, or other property; willful

trespasses, by cutting or destroying wood, timber, grain, and fruits, are offenses which subject the offender to severe penalties, as will be seen by reference to Chapter 245 of the Compiled Laws of 1871.

It is an offense for a person to have in his possession tools that are adapted and designed for use in breaking open buildings, vaults, safes, or other depositories in order to steal therefrom, and subjects the offender to imprisonment in the State Prison not more than ten years, or to a fine not exceeding one thousand dollars and imprisonment in the County Jail not more than one year.

Stealing property in another State and bringing it into this, subjects the offender to the same punishment as if the offense was committed in this State.

Willful or malicious injury to shade trees, where the damage amounts to twenty-five dollars, subjects the offender to imprisonment in the State Prison not exceeding five years, or to a fine not exceeding five hundred dollars, or to imprisonment in the County Jail not exceeding one year, at the discretion of the Court.

The removal or disposition of mortgaged property, with intent to defraud the person owning the mortgage, is a *misdemeanor*, and is punishable by fine not exceeding one hundred dollars, or by imprisonment in the County Jail not exceeding three months, or both.

Willfully destroying or removing timber from the lands of another, amounting to twenty-five dollars in value, subjects the offender to imprisonment in the State Prison not more than one year, or to a fine not more than five hundred dollars, or to imprisonment in the County Jail not more than one year. If the value of the timber or trees so taken is less than twenty-five dollars, the fine cannot exceed one hundred dollars, or the imprisonment three months in the County Jail.

To enter a vineyard during the months of August, September, or October, and eat or carry away any of the fruit therefrom, without the consent of the owner or occupant, is an offense, and the penalty a fine of five dollars, or twenty days' imprisonment in the County Jail, or both.

Questions—What is said of falsely personating another? Of obtaining property under false pretenses? Of the destruction and fitting out of vessels with certain intent? Of false invoice of cargo, or false protest? Of malicious injury to property? What is said of having burglar's tools in one's possession? Of stealing property in another State, and bringing it into this? What of injuries to shade trees? Of the destroying or removal of timber from others' lands? Of trespasses in vineyards?

CHAPTER LXVI.

OF OFFENSES UPON, AND IN RELATION TO RAILROADS AND CARS.

Any person who shall place upon any railroad any obstruction, or loosen, or displace any rail of the track of such railroad, or do any other act with intent to endanger the safety of any person traveling or being upon such railroad, or to throw from such railroad any locomotive, tender, or car, moving along the track of such railroad on which shall be any person, or property, liable to be injured thereby, shall be punished by imprisonment in the State Prison for life, or for a term of years.

Stealing from persons or cars while detained on account of accident or injury to such cars or to a railroad, subjects the offender to imprisonment in the State Prison not exceeding twenty years, or to a fine not exceeding three thousand dollars,

or both, at the discretion of the Court. Maliciously uncoupling, or detaching the locomotive, tender, or cars of any railroad train, or to aid, or abet in doing of the same, by persons
not in the employ of the railroad company, subjects the
offender to imprisonment in the State Prison not exceeding
ten years, or to a fine not exceeding two thousand dollars, or
both, at the discretion of the Court.

Seizing upon any locomotive with any express or mail car
thereto attached, and running away with the same, upon any
railroad, is a State Prison offense—term not to exceed ten
years—or the offender may be fined not exceeding two thousand dollars, or both, as the Court shall determine.

Questions—What is the law in relation to placing obstructions
upon railroads? Of stealing from cars, or persons when detained,
from injury or accident? Of uncoupling cars? Of stealing locomo-
tives?

CHAPTER LXVII.

OF FORGERY AND COUNTERFEITING.

Forgery consists in making something in the likeness of
something else, and designed to represent that which it is not.
It is defined in the law books as the "making of any written
instrument for the purpose of fraud and deceit." It may consist either in counterfeiting some writing or printed matter or
in setting a false name to it, to the prejudice of another. If
a signature to a paper be genuine, yet if the instrument written or printed over it is not authorized by the signer, the
forgery may be complete; or if the instrument be changed
without authority, after it has been executed, such change may
constitute a forgery.

The forging of instruments or records, designed to affect the legal rights of others, with intent to defraud or injure any person, subjects the offender, on conviction, to imprisonment in the State Prison not more than fourteen years, or in the County Jail not more than one year, depending upon the character of the instrument forged, and the circumstances surrounding the particular case.

The *uttering* or *publishing* of forged instruments is punishable the same as for the forgery.

If any person shall have in his possession at the same time, ten or more similar false, altered, forged, or counterfeit notes, bills of credit, bank bills, or notes, payable to the bearer thereof, or to the order of any person, knowing the same to be false, altered or counterfeit, with intent to utter the same as true, and to injure and defraud, he shall be punished by imprisonment in the State Prison not more than seven years, or in the County Jail not more than one year.

Every person is liable to be punished by imprisonment in the State Prison not more than ten years, or by fine not exceeding one thousand dollars and imprisonment in the County Jail not more than one year, who shall engrave, make, or mend, any instrument, or shall provide any material adapted or designed for the forging of notes, certificates, or other bills of credit, or the like, as specified in Chapter 246 of the Compiled Laws of Michigan of 1871, or who shall have such plates, or materials in his possession, with intent to use the same, or to permit them to be used in effecting such forgery.

Counterfeiting gold or silver coin, or having five or more pieces of false money, or coin, knowing the same to be counterfeit, and with intent to utter or pass the same as true, shall be punished by imprisonment in the State Prison for life, or for any number of years.

Any person having in his possession any number of pieces

less than five, of counterfeit coin, knowing the same to be counterfeit, with intent to pass the same as true, or passing, or offering to pass, any such coin, subjects the offender, on conviction, to imprisonment in the State Prison not more than ten years, or to a fine not exceeding one thousand dollars.

The making, or knowingly having in one's possession, tools for making counterfeit money, with the intent to use them, or to permit them to be used or employed in coining or making counterfeit money, subjects the offender on conviction, to imprisonment in the State Prison not more than ten years, or to a fine not exceeding one thousand dollars and imprisonment in the County Jail not more than one year.

Questions — What is forgery? What is the penalty for forgery? What is meant by the uttering or publishing of forged instruments? The penalty? What of having in one's possession forged notes, bank bills, etc.? What provision is made with reference to making or mending implements for making counterfeit bills, etc.? Of the law as to persons who have the possession of such tools? What is the law with reference to the counterfeiting of coin? Of having counterfeit coin in one's possession? What is said of the possession or manufacture of tools for counterfeiting?

CHAPTER LXVIII.

OF OFFENSES AGAINST PUBLIC JUSTICE.

PERJURY — BRIBERY — ESCAPE OF PRISONERS — DUTIES OF OFFICERS AND OTHERS IN ARRESTING OFFENDERS.

If any person authorized by the statute of this State to take an oath, or if any person of whom an oath shall be required by law, shall willfully swear falsely in regard to any matter or thing respecting which such oath is authorized or required, such person shall be deemed guilty of perjury.

The punishment for perjury, if committed on the trial of treason against the State, is imprisonment in the State Prison for life, or any term of years, and if committed in any other case, by imprisonment in the State Prison not more than fifteen years.

Persons who procure others to commit perjury are subject to the same penalty as those who commit perjury. If any person shall attempt, though unsuccessful, to induce a person to commit perjury, he shall be punished by imprisonment in the State Prison not more than five years, or imprisonment in the County Jail not more than one year.

To give or to offer to any Legislative, Judicial, or Executive officer any gift or gratuity, with intent to influence his official action, vote, or opinion, subjects the offender to imprisonment in the State Prison not more than five years, or to a fine not exceeding three thousand dollars and imprisonment in the County Jail not more than one year.

To accept a bribe, by such officers, with the understanding that his vote, decision, or opinion, shall be given in a particular manner, or upon a particular side of a question, subjects the offender to imprisonment in the State Prison not more than ten years, or to a fine not exceeding five thousand dollars and imprisonment in the County Jail not more than one year.

The giving, offering to, or taking bribes, by jurors or others, not included in the preceding paragraphs, who act in an official capacity, is punishable by imprisonment in the State Prison not exceeding five years, or by fine not exceeding one thousand dollars, or by imprisonment in the County Jail not more than one year.

Aiding persons lawfully imprisoned, or in custody, to escape, subjects the offender to severe punishment, depending upon the nature of the offense with which the prisoner is charged, and the manner in which such assistance is rendered. This punishment varies, and may be a fine not exceeding five hundred dollars, imprisonment in the County Jail not exceeding one year, and in some cases imprisonment in the State Prison not exceeding seven years.

Jailors and others, having the lawful custody of prisoners, are liable for voluntarily or negligently, permitting them to escape. If the act is willful, the officer is liable to suffer the like punishment as the person he permits to escape.

Officers required to arrest offenders or to serve any process, are subject to severe penalties and even imprisonment, in some cases, for two years in the County Jail, for refusing to make such arrest or serve such process. Sheriffs, Coroners, and Constables have a right to call upon any person or persons to assist them in the execution of their office, in any criminal case, or in the preservation of the peace, or the arresting of any person for a breach of the peace, or in case of escape of persons arrested upon civil process; and to refuse such assistance, subjects the offender, on conviction, to imprisonment in the County Jail not more than six months, or to a fine not exceeding one hundred dollars. The same penalty may be incurred by refusing to obey a Justice of the Peace, who may order the arrest of persons guilty of a breach of the peace.

Questions — What is perjury, under the statutes of Michigan? What is the penalty? What is said of procuring, or attempting to procure others to commit perjury? What is the law in relation to bribery? In relation to aiding prisoners to escape? Permitting them to escape? How may officers be punished for refusing to discharge certain duties? What right have certain officers to assistance? What is the penalty for a refusal to render such assistance, or to obey the order of a Justice of the Peace in relation to the arrest of disturbers of the peace?

CHAPTER LXIX.

OF CERTAIN OFFENSES — FALSELY ASSUMING TO BE A PUBLIC
OFFICER — CONCEALING OR COMPOUNDING OFFENSES —
EXTORTION BY OFFICERS — RESISTANCE TO OFFICERS —
RIOTS — MOLESTATION OF LABORERS.

If any person shall falsely take upon himself to act or
officiate in any office or place of authority, he shall be punished by imprisonment in the County Jail not more than one
year, or by fine not exceeding four hundred dollars.

Persons having knowledge of the commission of crimes,
who, for a consideration, conceal such knowledge, or who
attempt to settle and compromise such offense, so as to prevent a prosecution for the same, may be punished therefor —
the punishment being graded according to the nature of the
offense sought to be concealed or compromised, the highest
punishment being imprisonment in the State Prison for five
years. This, however, does not apply to cases of assault and
battery, and other misdemeanors, where the settlement is
effected by the injured party, who would have a remedy by a
civil action, for damages.

Officers who willfully and corruptly demand and receive
for their services more than the law allows, may be punished
for such extortion, by a fine not exceeding one hundred dollars.

Resistance to officers engaged in the discharge of their
duties, is an offense, and subjects the offender to imprisonment in the State Prison not to exceed two years, or imprisonment in the County Jail not to exceed one year, or to a fine not
exceeding five hundred dollars.

11

The assembling together of persons to disturb the peace and quiet of the people, or to engage in any unlawful conduct, is an offense. See Chapter 248 of the Compiled Laws of 1871.

Persons who, by threats, intimidations, or otherwise, without authority of law, interfere with and molest mechanics and other laborers in the quiet and peaceable pursuit of their *avocations*, may be punished by fine of not less than ten dollars, nor more than one hundred dollars, or by imprisonment in the County Jail not less than one month, nor more than one year, or by both fine and imprisonment, in the discretion of the Court.

Questions — What is the penalty for falsely assuming to be an officer? What provision is made to prevent the concealing of crime? What is the law in relation to extortion by officers? In relation to resistance to officers? What is said of riotous assemblies and of efforts to molest mechanics and laborers while at work?

CHAPTER LXX.

OFFENSES AGAINST CHASTITY, MORALITY, AND DECENCY.

Severe penalties are prescribed for offenses against chastity and decency. The punishment therefor will be found stated in Chapter 249 of the Compiled Laws of Michigan.

The ill effects of obscene books, or prints, upon the morals of those who allow themselves to read or even look upon them, is so apparent, that in most, if not all the States, heavy penalties have been provided for the punishment of those who distribute, or have in their possession, such books or prints.

In this State it is provided that if any person shall import, print, publish, sell or distribute any book, pamphlet, bal-laa, printed paper, or other things, containing obscene language, or obscene prints, pictures, figures, or descriptions manifestly tending to the corruption of the morals of youth, or shall introduce into any family, school, or place of education, or shall buy, procure, receive, or have in his possession, any such book, pamphlet, ballad, printed paper, or other things, either for the purpose of sale, exhibition, loan, or circulation, or with intent to introduce the same into any family, school, or place of education, shall be punished by imprisonment in the County Jail not more than one year, or by fine not exceeding one thousand dollars.

If any person shall willfully blaspheme the holy name of God, by cursing or *contumeliously reproaching* God, he shall be punished by imprisonment in the County Jail not more than six months, or by fine not exceeding fifty dollars.

If any person who has arrived at the age of discretion shall profanely curse or damn, or swear by the name of God, Jesus Christ, or the Holy Ghost, he shall, on conviction thereof, be punished by a fine not exceeding five dollars nor less than one dollar.

Disturbing religious, or other meetings, where the citizens are peaceably and lawfully assembled, is an offense punishable by fine or imprisonment in the County Jail.

Provision has been made by law to punish those who, without legal authority, dig up, disinter, or remove the dead body of any human being. The penalty provided, is imprisonment in the State Prison not more than one year, or in the County Jail not more than one year, or a fine not exceeding two thousand dollars.

It is provided that if any person shall willfully destroy, mutilate, deface, injure, or remove any tomb, monument, gravestone, or other structure or thing placed or designed for a memorial of the dead, or any fence, railing, curb, or other thing intended for the protection or for the ornament of any tomb, monument, gravestone, or other structure before mentioned, or of any inclosure for the burial of the dead, or shall willfully destroy, mutilate, remove, cut, break, or injure any tree, shrub, or plant, placed or being within any such inclosure, the person so offending shall be punished by a fine not exceeding five hundred dollars, nor less than ten dollars, or by imprisonment in the County Jail not more than one year.

Persons who engage in, or who aid, or encourage any prize-fight, are liable to be punished therefor by imprisonment in the State Prison not exceeding five years nor less than one year, or by fine not exceeding two thousand dollars, or by both fine and imprisonment, at the discretion of the Court. It is also unlawful to be present at such fight, or to give, or publish notice thereof, or to invite any person to attend such fight, under a penalty of imprisonment in the County Jail or in the Detroit House of Correction not exceeding one year, or a fine not exceeding five hundred dollars.

Selling unwholesome provisions without notice of their character to the buyer ; *adulterating* food, liquors, drugs, or medicines, are offenses subjecting the offender to a fine or imprisonment in the County Jail.

Persons who sell poisons are required to affix to the vial, box, or parcel containing the same, a label which shall contain the true name of the article sold, and also the word "Poison." A failure to comply with this provision, subjects the offender to a fine not exceeding one hundred dollars. Persons selling poisons are also required, under a penalty not exceeding fifty dollars, to keep a record of the date of all such sales, the article and the amount thereof, and the person or persons to whom delivered, and their residence.

If any person shall put the carcass of any dead animal, in any place within one mile of the residence of any person, except the same be buried at least two feet under ground, and permit the same to remain there to the injury or annoyance of the citizens, he shall, on conviction, be punished by a fine of not less than five nor more than ten dollars and costs.

Questions — What chapter of the Compiled Laws treats of offenses against chastity? What provision of law is made with reference to obscene books and prints? What is the law in relation to blasphemy? The penalty for profane swearing? For disturbance of meetings, &c? For violation of *sepulture?* For injuring tombs and memorials of the dead? What is the law in relation to prize-fighting? Selling unwholesome provisions? Adulterating food, liquors, &c.? What provision is made concerning the selling of poisons? In relation to the burial of dead animals?

CHAPTER LXXI.

OF OFFENSES AGAINST PUBLIC POLICY — LOTTERIES — TELEGRAPHIC MESSAGES — OFFENSES AGAINST ELECTION LAWS — CRUELTY TO ANIMALS.

It is unlawful to set up and promote, or in any way to aid or be concerned in the setting up, managing or drawing of any lottery, or gift enterprise, or to sell tickets therefor ; and it is provided that persons guilty of such offense shall be punished by a fine not exceeding two thousand dollars, or by imprisonment in the County Jail not more than one year.

Telegraphic Messages. — Any person connected with any telegraphic company in this State, who shall willfully divulge the contents, or the nature of the contents of any private communication intrusted to him or her, for transmission or delivery, or who shall willfully refuse or neglect to transmit or deliver the same, shall, on conviction therefor, suffer impris-

onment in the county jail or work-house in the county where
such conviction shall be had, for a term of not more than three
months, or shall pay a fine not to exceed five hundred dollars,
in the discretion of the Court.

Offenses Against Election Laws. — Officers who willfully
neglect their duties under the election laws, or who are guilty
of corrupt conduct in executing the same, are liable to imprisonment in the State Prison not exceeding three years, or to a
fine not exceeding one thousand dollars.

Persons who by any corrupt means attempt to influence
an elector in giving his vote, are liable to a fine not exceeding
five hundred dollars, or to imprisonment in the County Jail
not exceeding one year, or both, as the Court shall direct.

Persons who vote without a legal right to do so, and persons who attempt to persuade others to vote when they have
no legal right to vote, may be fined, not exceeding five hundred dollars, or be imprisoned in the County Jail not exceeding one year, or both, in the discretion of the Court.

Persons unlawfully interfering with any ballot-box, during
the progress of an election, and before the ballots are counted
and the result declared, or who shall fraudulently or forcibly
add to or diminish the number of ballots legally deposited,
and all persons aiding or abetting therein, shall be adjudged
guilty of a misdemeanor, and on conviction thereof, shall be
punished by imprisonment in the State Prison for a term not
exceeding ten years, or by a fine not exceeding one thousand
dollars.

Cruelty to Animals. — Persons guilty of cruelty to animals may be punished by imprisonment in the County Jail
not exceeding one year, or by fine not exceeding two hundred and fifty dollars, or both. Such cruelty may consist in
over-driving, over-loading, want of food, drink, or shelter,
want of protection from the weather, beating or mutilating,

or in any other way by which the animal is tortured or tormented.

Keeping a place for the purpose of fighting or baiting animals, is a misdemeanor.

The law forbids the carrying of live animals with their legs tied together, or in any cruel and inhuman manner.

Railroad companies are not permitted to keep live animals in their cars for a longer period than twenty-eight *consecutive* hours, without unloading them for rest, water, and feeding, for a period of at least five consecutive hours, unless prevented from so unloading, by storm, or other accidental cause.

Setting Fire to Woods, &c. — Every person who shall willfully or negligently set fire to any woods, prairies, or grounds, not his own property, or shall willfully or negligently permit any fire to pass from his own woods, prairies or grounds, to the injury or destruction of the property of any other person, may be fined not exceeding one thousand dollars, or be imprisoned in the County Jail not exceeding one year, or both, in the discretion of the Court ; and shall be liable to the party injured in double the amount of damages sustained.

Questions—What is the law as to lotteries? Disclosing of the contents of telegraphic messages? What is the punishment for negligence or corruption on the part of election officers? For improperly influencing voters? For voting without legal authority, or attempting to persuade others to do so? What is said as to interfering with the ballot box? What is the penalty for cruelty to animals? Mention some of the acts or omissions constituting cruelty? What is said as to the manner of carrying animals? What is required of railroad companies carrying live stock? State what is said as to setting fire to woods, prairies, or other grounds?

UNITED STATES CAPITOL.

GOVERNMENT OF THE UNITED STATES.

CHAPTER I.

In the early history of this country the people were *subjects* of the British Empire. Extensive grants of territory were conferred upon individuals and companies. Some of these grants conferred certain powers of government. Out of these grants Colonies were organized, with *charters* specifying what governmental powers might be exercised. They authorized the establishment of Legislatures to make laws for the government of the people, provided such laws should not conflict with the laws of the British Parliament.

Governors for the Colonies were appointed by the King of England, in whom was vested executive authority.

The Colonies, while subject to Great Britain, were entirely independent of each other.

In course of time the British Government became *exacting* and oppressive towards the Colonies, denying them many of the privileges that had been granted by their charters.

In 1765, at the request of the Massachusetts Legislature, the different Colonies sent representatives, or *delegates*, to meet in convention to counsel together concerning their difficulties with the British Government. In the same year delegates from nine Colonies met in New York, and agreed upon, and signed *petitions* and *memorials* representing their grounds of complaint, and forwarded them to the King.

September 5, 1774, delegates from eleven of the Colonies met at Philadelphia. This body was called the Continental Congress. It adjourned in October, to meet again in May, 1775. Various measures were adopted designed to protect the people against the *encroachments* of the mother country, and on the 4th of July, 1776, Congress declared the Colonies to be free and independent States.

Thus far, no provision had been made for incorporating the States into one nation for the purposes of government ; but believing it to be necessary for their mutual protection and safety, in November, 1776, a plan of union was agreed upon. This plan was set out in a writing called, " Articles of *Confederation* and perpetual union between the States," and was to become operative, that is, go into effect, when adopted by the Legislatures of all the States.

In 1778, the articles were adopted by eleven of the States ; in 1779, by one, and by the thirteenth and last, in 1781. So that, on the 23d of March, 1781, the new government went into operation, under the name of the United States of America.

It was soon found that the Articles of Confederation did not confer sufficient power upon the National Government, to make it *effective*. Its powers were vested in Congress ; and no provision had been made for an executive or a judicial department. It could pass laws, but could not enforce them. It could determine how many men and how much money each State should furnish to carry on the war, but it was left for the States to execute the law. If they refused, there was no law to compel them to comply. To defray the expenses of the war, Congress borrowed large sums of money; several millions of which was from Holland and France.

Another difficulty arose from the fact that different States enacted laws giving their own citizens undue advantages over the citizens of other States.

To enable the National Government to control, in needful cases, the action of the States, it was found necessary to confer greater powers upon it. So, in May, 1787, delegates chosen by all the States, except Rhode Island, assembled at Philadelphia, and adopted our present constitution. This was submitted to the people of the States for their approval.

The people chose delegates in each State to attend State Conventions, with power to approve or reject the proposed constitution. These Conventions approved the constitution, and thus our present Government was established.

The Constitution of the United States may be said to be an agreement of the different States with each other, as to the form and powers of the National Government. It confers certain powers of government and control over the States and the people of the United States. Hence, we refer to the Constitution and the Government as the *Federal* Constitution, or the Federal Government.

Questions — Of what Government were the people of this country formerly subjects? What is said of the organization of Colonies? Who appointed the Governors? What action was taken by the Colonies in 1765? In 1774? In 1776? When were the Articles of Confederation adopted? What powers had the Government under the Articles of Confederation? What was the occasion for a change in the government? How, and when was this change effected? What is said of the Constitution of the United States?

CHAPTER II.

The Executive Department of the Government is vested in the President. The duties of the President and Vice-President are similar to those of the Governor and Lieutenant-Governor of a State. The President appoints the officers necessary to assist him in executing the laws.

Most of the executive business is done through departments; and each department has a head officer, called a Secretary.

The Secretary of State performs for the National Government duties similar to those performed by the State Secretaries, for the States; and in addition thereto, he has charge of our affairs with foreign nations, and gives directions, under the President, to our foreign Ministers and Consuls.

The Secretary of the Treasury has charge of, and conducts the *financial* affairs of the Government. Amongst other things, it is his duty to attend to the collection of funds for the support of the Government; to make out and report to Congress, estimates of the public *revenues* and expenses, and to inform that body what appropriations will be needed for the use of the Government.

The Secretary of War has charge of the Military Department.

The Secretary of the Navy has the charge of the business relating to the Navy.

The Attorney-General is the legal adviser of the President and heads of the various Departments, and prosecutes suits in the Supreme Court of the United States.

The Postmaster-General has the general supervision of postoffices, and of the carrying and distributing of the mails.

The Secretary of the Interior has charge of the Indian, land, pension, and patent matters.

The heads of these several Departments constitute the President's Cabinet, and are his counsellors and advisers.

Questions — In whom is the Executive Department of the United States vested ? Does the President execute the laws in person ? How does he execute them ? Name the chief department officers. What are the duties of each ?

CHAPTER III.

LEGISLATIVE DEPARTMENT OF THE GOVERNMENT OF THE UNITED STATES.

The Legislative Department is vested in Congress, consisting of two bodies: a Senate and House of Representatives.

The Senate has two members from each State, who are elected for six years.

The Vice-President is the presiding officer of the Senate.

The advice and consent of the Senate is necessary for the appointment of many of the officers of the Government.

When charges are preferred against certain officers of the United States, the Senate tries them; and when sitting for that purpose, is a Court of Impeachment. The Chief Justice of the Supreme Court presides on such occasions.

In matters of legislation, the proceedings of the two Houses of Congress are similar to those of the two branches of the State Legislature. The members of the House of Representatives hold their offices for two years. The States are divided into districts, and a member is elected in each district.

The powers of Congress are delegated to it by the Constitution; and in this respect it differs from the State Legislatures. The State Constitutions prescribe and indicate what the Legislatures may not do; the Federal Constitution declares what Congress may do. Hence, in determining whether an act of Congress is constitutional, the question is, " Does the Constitution authorize the act?"—and in determining whether an act of a State Legislature is constitutional, the question is, " Does the Constitution forbid it?"

Questions — In what body is the Legislative Department of the Government vested? How many members has the Senate? Mention some of the duties of the Senate, not pertaining to the ordinary matters of legislation. How are members of the House elected? How long is their term of office? What is said of the powers of Congress? In what respect do the powers of Congress differ from the powers of the State Legislatures? What is the test of the constitutionality of an act?

CHAPTER IV.

JUDICIAL DEPARTMENT OF THE GOVERNMENT OF THE UNITED STATES.

The Federal Constitution provides that the Judicial power of the United States shall be vested in one Supreme Court, and such inferior Courts as Congress may, from time to time, establish. It also enumerates the duties and powers of these Courts.

The Supreme Court consists of nine members.

The United States is divided into ten Circuits, and a Judge is appointed in each Circuit. The Circuit Courts revise the decisions of the District Courts, and in addition to certain civil causes they may try, they have jurisdiction for the trial of the highest crimes against the United States. When a Justice of the Supreme Court of the United States is present at a Circuit Court, he presides. The Judge of a District Court sometimes sits with the Circuit Judge, in which case the Circuit Judge presides.

District Courts are established throughout the United States. In each State there is at least one District Court. This Court has jurisdiction in admiralty, bankruptcy, and many other cases. It also has jurisdiction over offenses against the laws of the United States.

In addition to these, Congress has established a Court of Claims, for the adjudication of claims against the Government.

Questions — What provision is made in the Constitution for the establishment of Courts? Of how many members is the Supreme Court composed? How many Circuit Courts are there in the United States? What is said of the jurisdiction of Circuit Courts? What Judge presides in the Circuit Court? What is said of the establishment of District Courts? Of their jurisdiction? Of the Court of Claims?

APPENDIX.

Abscond, to hide, or secrete one's self.

Acquiescence, compliance, consent.

Action, legal demand of one's rights, in court, or, a crim-inal prosecution.

Adhering, to remain with, to take sides with.

Adjust, to regulate, put in order.

Administer, to supply, to act as an agent in doing a thing, or, enforcing a law or the like.

Administration, the act of administering.

Admissibility, proper, or worthy to be admitted.

Adulterating, corrupting, polluting, debasing.

Adultery, sexual intercourse between a married person and one to whom such person is not married.

Affidavit, an oath in writing.

Affirmation, confirmation, declaration.

Affirm, to declare, tell or indorse confidently.

Aforesaid, said before, named before.

Aggregate, the sum or result of various particulars.

Agreement, compact, bargain.

Agriculture, tillage, husbandry, cultivation of the soil.

Alderman, an officer of an incorporated town, an incor-porated magistrate.

Alien, a foreigner who has not been naturalized.

Allegiance, the duty of a subject.

Allegations, affirmations, statements or pleas.

Amulet, an ornament, gem, scroll or the like, worn as a charm to prevent disease or other injury.

12

Ancestor, one from whom a person descends—one from whom an inheritance is derived.

Apparent, plain, evident, certain.

Apparatus, tools or instruments for any trade.

Appendix, addition, supplement.

Apportion, to divide into just parts.

Apprentice, one bound to serve a tradesman.

Appropriate, to assign to any particular use, to make use of — fit, proper.

Appurtenance, that which belongs to something else.

Arms, weapons.

Artificial, made by art, not natural.

Assault, to attack, invade.

Assemble, to meet together, or call together.

Assign, to make out, transfer.

Atrocious, wicked, heinous, enormous.

Avocation, employment.

Bailee, one to whom goods are intrusted.

Bar, to prevent, prohibit.

Battery, an unlawful touching of another's person.

Beverage, liquor for drinking to gratify appetite, or quench thirst.

Bind out. These words refer to the agreement by which a person is held to service by another.

Board, several persons united to discharge some duty prescribed by law.

Body Politic, the people united together for the purpose of government.

Breach of trust, misappropriation of a thing that has been intrusted to another in confidence.

Breviary, a book containing the service of the Roman Catholic or Greek Church.

Candidate, one who asks for a place.

Cassock, a cloak or gown worn over other garments.

Certify, to give certain information.

Certiorari, to be certified to — the name of a writ commanding an inferior court to certify and return the record of its proceedings to a higher court.

Chancery, a court of equity and conscience.

Character, one's moral state or condition, reputation.

Charter, a privilege granted by the government.

Civilized, polished, improved, civil.

Classify, to range in order, grade, or rank.

Classification, the act of forming into classes.

Cohabitation, living together.

Command, to order, govern, overlook.

Common-law, rules of action founded on long usage and the decisions of courts of justice, in distinction from the statute or written law.

Common-law jurisdiction, not confined, in the exercise of jurisdiction, exclusively to the statutes or written laws [See Common-law].

Community, the body politic.

Commutation, alteration, to exchange, or substitute, one thing for another.

Compensation, recompense.

Committed, sent to prison.

Complaint, an accusation.

Confederation, a compact for mutual support or protection.

Conferred, bestowed.

Conflict, disagreement.

Conjunction, united, associated, union.

Convention, an assembly of delegates, or representatives, to accomplish some specific object.

Consecutive, following in regular order.

Conscientious, just, exact; disposition to be and do right.

Contagious, infectious, catching.

Contumeliously, with reproach, contempt, insolently.

Convene, to call together, to assemble.

Contract, bargain, agreement.

Costs, expenses of a suit, which may be recovered from the losing party.

Countersign, the signature of a secretary or other subordinate officer to a writing signed by the principal or superior, to attest its authenticity.

Crime, an offense against public law. The word is generally used to indicate a felony.

Cultivate, to improve.

Deceased, departed from life, dead.
Decrepit, wasted and worn by age.
Deem, to judge, to conclude, to think.
Deface, to destroy, to raze, to disfigure.
Default, an omission, defect, failure.
Defendant, the person prosecuted.
Defraud, to rob by a trick, to cozen.
Delegate, an agent, to depute, commissioner.
Deliberate, to consider with care.
Dependent, reliance upon, or in the power of another.
Department, separate office, a division of the government.
Descent, coming down, derivation, or from an ancestor.
Designate, to point out, to distinguish.
Detention, the act of detaining, restraining.
Devise, the act of giving or disposing of real estate by a will.
Diagram, a figure or drawing.
Diploma, a document conferred by an educational institution, certifying to a degree of attainment or advancement in scholarship.
Discipline, to educate, to keep in order.
Discretion, prudence, liberty of action.
Disfigure, to deform, deface, mangle.
Diversion, turning aside from any course, occupation, or object.
Division, to divide, to set apart.
Domestic, belonging to the house, or home, or family.
Draft, to draw by lot; also, a bill drawn on another for money.
Duplicate, an exact copy of anything.
Duress, imprisonment or restraint.

Effective, able, efficient, active.
Elector [see page 42].
Eligible, fit to be chosen, possessing the requisite legal qualifications.
Enactment, to establish by law.
Encroachment, intruding upon the rights of others.
Ensue, to follow, to succeed.

Entitled, having a right to.

Equity, justice, right, honesty, impartiality.

Equitable, in an impartial manner.

Erection, a building.

Escheat, property that falls to the State, for want of any person to inherit it.

Essential, necessary, very important.

Established, settled, firmly fixed, located.

Estate, the interest or right one has in a thing, property.

Estate of inheritance, a perpetuity in lands to a man and his heirs ; or it is the right to succeed to the estate of a person who died without having made a will.

Estimate, to rate, to set a value, or price upon; to calculate.

Exacting, to force, to extort, to enjoin.

Exempt, to free from, to privilege.

Extraordinary, not common, unusual.

Expedient, proper, convenient, fitness.

Explorers, those who search through, or travel over, for the purpose of discovery.

Facilitate, to make clear, or easy.

Federal, pertaining to an agreement between parties, a compact.

Felony, a crime punishable by death, or imprisonment in the State Prison.

Filed, deposited with the proper officer.

Fish weir, a dam built to stop and raise the water for the taking of fish.

Fisheries, a place for propagating fish.

Flume, the passage or channel for the water which propels the wheel of a mill.

Forfeit, a penalty for an offense.

Forfeiture, the act of forfeiting ; a fine.

Foreigners, persons of other countries.

Fraudulently, by fraud, treacherously.

Freeman, one who enjoys liberty, or one who is not subject to the will of another ; one who enjoys, or is entitled to, a franchise, or privilege.

Fuel, material used for fire.

Fundamental, foundation, original, essential.

Govern, to control, or regulate.

Grade, rank, to arrange by degrees.

Grant, gift, to bestow, a conveyance.

Guest, visitor, one entertained.

Guide, to direct; as a noun it is one who directs.

Guide-board, a board containing directions to travelers.

Guide-post, a post containing directions to travelers.

Habitually, customarily, by habit.

Heirs, one who inherits by law, a successor.

Heinous, very wicked, atrocious.

Hereditament, anything that may be inherited, whether real, personal, or mixed.

Hospital, a building in which the sick or infirm are received and treated.

Hospitality, liberality in entertaining.

Householder, the head of a family in possession of a house.

Impeachment, a written accusation by the House of Representatives of the United States to the Senate of the United States against an officer. The lower Houses of State Legislatures also present articles of impeachment to the Senates against State officers for misconduct.

Importation, act of bringing from abroad, from without the State.

Impotent, incapacity to propagate the species.

Impressment, the act of seizing for public use, or of impressing into the public service.

Incur, to become liable to.

Incorporated [see page 76].

Infantry, the foot soldiers of an army.

Indigent, poor, having but little, if any property.

Infected, tainted, poisoned, polluted.

Infirmity, weakness, failing, disease.

Inhabitant, one who has a fixed residence in a place.

Inheritance [see estate of inheritance].

Inscription, a title, name, or character.

Inserted, placed among other things.

Installments, the parts of a debt due at different times.

Instituted, established, fixed.

Instrument, a writing containing the particulars of some act, contract, writ, or proceeding.

Insurrection, a rebellion of citizens, or subjects of a country, against its government.

Intermarry, to become connected by marriage.

Intersect, to cut into, or cross each other.

In transitu. Things are *in transitu* during their removal from one place to another.

Invalid, without legal force, or effect.

Invasion, the entry of a country by a public enemy, making war.

Issue, the point or question in controversy between con-tending parties. When applied to the descent of estates, it includes all the lawful, lineal descendants of the ancestor.

Jesuit, one of a religious order, of the Roman Catholic Church, founded by Ignatius Loyola, and approved in 1540, under the title of The Society of Jesus. The members take three vows : poverty, chastity, and obedience.

Juggler, one who plays tricks.

Jurisdiction, legal authority, a district.

Juvenile, youthful, young.

Kindre.', relatives by blood or marriage, more properly the former.

Larceny, stealing, theft.

Lascivious, lustful, lewd.

Lessee, one who takes an estate by lease.

Levy, the act of raising money or men ; to collect.

Lewd, disposition for lust.

Libel, a defamatory publication, satire.

Lien, a charge upon property, for the payment of a debt.

License, an authority given to do an act, which without such authority would be illegal.

Lieu, in place of, instead of.

Limit, to restrict.

Limitations, restrictions.

Lineal, descending in a direct line from an ancestor.

List, a roll, or catalogue.

Lock, the barrier, or works which confine the water of a stream or canal.

Magazine, a store-house.

Maliciously, with the spirit and intention of harm and mischief.

Mayor, a chief magistrate of a city.

Maim, to wound, cripple.

Malice, a spirit desiring harm, without just cause.

Mechanical, skilled in mechanics.

Memorial, something to preserve memory.

Menace, to threaten.

Michilimackinac, probably derives its name from the Indian words Michi-Mackinac, meaning a great truth, or from the Chippewa words Michine-Maukinonk, meaning the place of giant fairies.

Mile-board, a board on which distances are indicated.

Mile-stone, a stone on which distances are indicated.

Minor, one not of legal age to make a binding contract — smaller, less important.

Misdemeanor, an offense less heinous than a crime.

Mission, a station or residence for missionaries.

Missionary, one who is sent upon a mission; especially, one sent to propagate religion.

Mode, form, fashion.

Moral, just, honest, upright.

Monument, a pillar, statue, or other thing, to perpetuate the memory of a thing or person; a landmark.

Mountebank, a quack, a stage doctor.

Mustering, assembling, reviewing, collecting, or registering forces.

Municipal, belonging to a corporation.

Natural Science, the science of nature, as distinguished from the art or skill of man.

Native. All persons born in the United States are considered as natives.

Negotiable, that which may be transferred by assignment.

Non-resident, one who does not reside on his own lands.

Nuisance, something noxious or offensive.

Oath, a solemn affirmation which God is called upon to witness.

Obligation, agreement, contract, bond.

Offal, waste meat, refuse, unfit for use.

Office, a public employment.

Officer, one engaged in a public employment.

Offense, transgression, injury, violation of law.

Operative, having the power of acting.

Organized, formed, arranged.

Pardon, forgiveness, remission.

Parental, pertaining to parents.

Pauper, a poor person who receives alms, or is supported at the public charge.

Pecuniary, pertaining to money.

Penalty, a punishment, forfeiture.

Personate, to counterfeit, to represent.

Pertain, to belong, to relate.

Permanent, lasting, unchanged.

Personal Property, temporary and movable property.

Perjury [see page 158].

Petitions, requests, entreaties.

Plaintiff, the party who commences a suit.

Plurality, a greater number than some other, but not a majority of all.

Political, pertaining to a regular system or administration of government.

Polygamy, having more than one wife, or husband.

Posthumous children, those born after the death of the father, or taken from the dead body of the mother.

Premeditated, to think beforehand.

Preceding, to go before in rank or time.

Prescribe, to order, direct.

Principal, chief.

Prior, antecedent, former, anterior.

Provocation, a cause of anger.

Provided, stipulated as a condition, on condition.

Proving, evincing, ascertaining as truth.

Professional, relating to a profession.

Propagate, to generate, increase.

Process, a writ issued out of a court.

Proficiency, improvement.

Protest, a declaration against a thing; a written declaration of the master of a vessel that an injury to it was not occasioned by his fault.

Prothonotary, a register or chief clerk of a court, in particular States.

Punt-gun, a small cannon, carried on a flat-bottomed boat, and usually used for sporting.

Puppet-Show, mock play by images.

Qualified, made fit; accomplished.

Quorum, a sufficient number to transact business.

Range, to place in order, ranks.

Real property, lands.

Rebellion, insurrection by the people against their own country.

Reclaim, reform, correct, recall.

Recover, to win back, to gain as a compensation.

Relatively, having relation to something else.

Relevant, relative to, relating to.

Renounce, disavow.

Reproaching, censuring, upbraiding.

Representations, representing, describing, showing.

Reprieve, to respite from punishment.

Restrain, to withhold, repress, limit.

Resident, dwelling in a place.

Resident freeholder, one who resides on an estate of inheritance, or for life.

Resolution, that which is determined or decided.

Resort, to go to, or repair to; a place of assembling.

Resource, an expedient, a resort.

Respond, to answer, to accord or comply with.

Restrictions, confinement, limitations.

Revenues, income of a State, duties, taxes.

Rob, to take property from the person of another forcibly, feloniously, or by putting in fear.

Secular, pertaining to worldly matters.

Second, a supporter, next to the first.
Sepulture, interment, burial.
Seize, to take forcible possession of.
Seized, taken forcible possession of; to be possessed of.
Shute, a passage for fish through a dam or lock.
Signature, mark, sign, written name.
Simultaneous, existing or happening at the same time.
Site, situation, local position.
Slander, false report, to back-bite, to scandalize.
Specific, definite, particular quality, or sort.
Spawn, the eggs of fish.
Stipulation, agreement.
Subdivided, divided again.
Subject, one owing allegiance to a sovereign or government; to make liable to.
Subordinate, inferior in order.
Supremacy, higher authority or power.
Supervisory, to oversee, as an overseer, a superintendent.
Suppression, the act of subduing, or crushing.
Survey, to view, measure, examine.
Surrender, to yield, to give one's self up.
Surplus, excess, remainder.
Swivel-gun, a small cannon, carrying a shot of half a pound, made to turn in a swivel or socket, in any direction.

Tare, deficiency in the weight or quantity of goods by reason of the weight of the cask, box, or other thing containing the commodity and which is weighed with it.
Tax, toll, tribute, impost, custom or contribution for the service of the State.
Tenement, any species of permanent property that may be held so as to create a tenancy, as lands, houses, rents, etc.
Temporary, transient, for a short time.
Testamentary, pertaining to a will.
Territorial, pertaining to territory.
Token, mark, sign.
Transmit, to send from one person or place to another.
Treason [See page 147].
Trespass, unlawful entry upon the lands of another; to intrude upon the rights of another.

Tribunal, court of justice.
Tribe, a certain generation of people.

Usurpation, illegal possession.
Uttering or *publishing,* to hold out or pretend that the thing offered is good and genuine, when it is not.

Vagrant, an idle wanderer, a vagabond.
Vested, belonging to, having by right.
Veto, from the Latin, meaning "I forbid."
Violate, to infringe, injure, or break.
Void, having no legal or binding force.
Volunteers, those who join the military or naval forces voluntarily, of their own free will.

Ward, a minor, or person under the care of a guardian; subdivision of a city.
Warrant, an instrument authorizing an officer to seize an offender and bring him to justice; that which warrants or authorizes; to insure; guaranty, security.
Weir dam, a dam constructed to stop and raise the water for conducting it to a mill, for taking fish and the like.
Will, testament, the disposition of a man's estate.
Willful, obstinate, perverse, not yielding to reason.

INDEX.

[The reference figures are to the pages.]